# Web-Teaching

## A Guide to Designing Interactive Teaching for the World Wide Web

INNOVATIONS IN SCIENCE EDUCATION AND TECHNOLOGY

Series Editor:

Karen C. Cohen, Harvard University, Cambridge, Massachusetts

---

**The Hidden Curriculum—Faculty-Made Tests in Science**
**Part 1: Lower-Division Courses**
**Part 2: Upper-Division Courses**
Sheila Tobias and Jacqueline Raphael

**Internet Links for Science Education: Student–Scientist Partnerships**
Edited by Karen C. Cohen

**Web-Teaching: A Guide to Designing Interactive Teaching for the World Wide Web**
David W. Brooks

A Continuation Order Plan is available for this series. A continuation order will bring delivery of each new volume immediately upon publication. Volumes are billed only upon actual shipment. For further information please contact the publisher.

# Web-Teaching

## A Guide to Designing Interactive Teaching for the World Wide Web

David W. Brooks

University of Nebraska – Lincoln
Lincoln, Nebraska

PLENUM PRESS • NEW YORK AND LONDON

Library of Congress Cataloging-in-Publication Data

Brooks, David W.
    Web-teaching : a guide to designing interactive teaching for the
World Wide Web / David W. Brooks.
        p.   cm. -- (Innovations in science education and technology)
    Includes bibliographical references and index.
    ISBN 0-306-45552-8
    1. Teaching--Computer network resources.  2. World Wide Web
(Information retrieval system)  3. Interactive multimedia.
4. Science--Study and teaching--Computer network resources.
I. Title.  II. Series.
LB1044.87.B76  1997
025.06'371102--dc21                                           97-1861
                                                                  CIP

ISBN 0-306-45552-8

© 1997 Plenum Press, New York
A Division of Plenum Publishing Corporation
233 Spring Street, New York, N.Y. 10013

http://www.plenum.com

10 9 8 7 6 5 4

Printed in the United States of America

To Helen, Dan, and Eileen
for their love and understanding


To Frank Collea and Al Kilgore
for their leadership and support

# PREFACE TO THE SERIES

The mandate to expand and improve science education for the 21st century is global and strong. Implementing these changes, however, is very complicated given that science education is dynamic, continually incorporating new ideas, practices, and procedures. Lacking clear paths for improvement, we can and should learn from the results of all types of science education, traditional as well as experimental. Thus, successful reform of science education requires careful orchestration of a number of factors. Technological developments, organizational issues, and teacher preparation and enhancement, as well as advances in the scientific disciplines themselves, must all be taken into account. The current prospects look bright given national reform movements such as the National Academy of Science's "Standards for Science Education" and the American Association for the Advancement of Science's "Benchmarks"; the backing of science education leadership; and recent developments, including the Internet and new educational software. Further, we have a world-wide citizenry more alert to the need for quality science education for all students, not just those who will become scientists. If we can isolate and combine such factors appropriately, we will have levers for science education reform. The books in this series deal in depth with these factors, these potential levers for science education reform.

In 1992, a multidisciplinary forum was launched for sharing the perspectives and research findings of the widest possible community of people involved in addressing the challenge. All who had something to share regarding impacts on science education were invited to contribute. This forum was the *Journal of Science Education and Technology*. Since the inception of the journal, many articles have highlighted relevant themes and topics: the role and importance of technology, organizational structure, human factors, legislation, philosophical and pedagogical movements, and advances in the scientific disciplines themselves. In addition, approaches to helping teachers learn about and use multimedia materials and the Internet have been reported. This series of volumes will treat in depth consistently recurring topics that can support and sustain the scientific education enterprise and be used to raise levels of scientific knowledge and involvement for all.

The first four volumes illustrate the variety and potential of these factors. *The Hidden Curriculum—Faculty-Made Tests in Science: Part 1, Lower Division Courses* and *The Hidden Curriculum—Faculty-Made Tests in Science: Part 2, Upper Division Courses* are premised on the belief that testing practices influence educational procedures and learning outcomes. Innovations in exam practices that assess scientific understanding in new and more appropriate ways should be shared with the widest possible audience. The research described and the resulting compendium of hundreds of contributed, annotated best exam practices in all science courses at the college level is a resource for every science educator and administrator.

*Web-Teaching: A Guide to Designing Interactive Teaching for the World Wide Web* aids instructors in developing and using interactive, multimedia educational materials on the World Wide Web. It also helps instructors organize and control these resources for their students' use. Not only do instructors learn how to improve their own materials and delivery, but they can access and make available Web-based information in a way their students can comprehend and master. Using the lever of instructional technology is an increasingly important part of science teaching; this book guides that process.

Finally, *Internet Links for Science Education: Student–Scientist Partnerships* illustrates the workings and effectiveness of this new paradigm and growing force in science education. In these partnerships (SSPs), students help scientists answer questions that could never before be fully addressed due to the lack of a large number of strategically positioned observers. Students gather and analyze data in projects involving authentic and important scientific questions, and science teachers actively explain science to students and help scientists implement their research. Data gathering and sharing, the heart of effective SSPs, is possible and rapid with the help of the Internet and a variety of technologies—groupware, visualization, imaging, and others. Several representative SSPs are described in depth. Chapters on student data and the human and technological infrastructures required to support SSPs help readers understand the interplay of the several factors in this approach to improving science education K–12. The Appendix contains a useful annotated list of current projects with complete contact information. Readers of this book will come away with an understanding of these programs from multiple perspectives and will be encouraged to become involved in similar efforts.

It is our hope that each book in the series will be a resource for those who are part of the science reform effort.

Karen C. Cohen
Cambridge, Massachusetts

# PREFACE

This book deals with using the kinds of hardware, software, and networks commonly used on the World Wide Web (WWW) to deliver and support instruction and learning.

When the opportunity presented itself to write a book on multimedia and science teaching, I took it gladly. I've had an unusual career. I was trained as a chemist by Joe Gettler at New York University and Charles Dawson at Columbia. Even while still a junior at NYU, my interests turned toward chemistry education. By the time I was tenured, I had decided to devote full time to chem ed — against the wise counsel of many friends and colleagues.

My early experiences were based on very large classes and multisection courses with thousands of students. In fact, in my last semester as a chemistry coordinator, I supervised more teaching assistants than students I've ever had in any semester since becoming a full-time Professor of Curriculum and Instruction! With large enrollments in multisection courses, it is not surprising that course coordinators turn toward multimedia. I've worked with multimedia intensively since 1968, my first year as coordinator of a large, multisection course.

After graduate school, I never used computers for much other than recordkeeping. I did use a wonderful and powerful but obscure computer language, APL, to develop some management tools for large multisection chemistry programs. My first introduction to desktop machines came with the early IBMs around 1980. A rapid conversion put me on a path toward Macintosh in early 1988; I was fully converted by June of that year. I can't tell you how much I look forward to a common platform.

My introduction to the World Wide Web came from Paul Kramer who demonstrated *Mosaic* to a Nebraska faculty group a few years ago. I confess to being impressed and unimpressed at the same time. Everything seemed quite good except for the very slow speed and substantial system instability. *Netscape* changed that. By late summer of 1995, I had set up my first server. I'd been a "paperless" professor for several years, having switched to 3.5-inch disks a decade ago. The Web was even better. In addition to text and images, I was able to use the WWW to distribute software from my course pages.

The last thing I thought possible would be for instructional costs to go down — in any subject. WWW instruction seems to be *less* expensive for institutions than conventional instruction in many areas. Wow! That is a very scary thought.

When asked to write a book that looks ahead into a fast-moving system in transition, I decided to work in two areas. One was to give readers an idea of the nature of the pieces currently available for instructors to play with when delivering Web-based teaching. The other was to try to assemble sufficient resources from teaching and learning research such that those teachers could begin with instructional designs likely to be effective.

Chapter 1 is an introduction that summarizes these views in some detail. Chapter 2 includes potentially useful research on teaching and learning. It may surprise many readers to learn that support for multimedia or learning styles is much weaker than many think it is, but that support for cooperative learning seems very strong.

Chapter 3, "Multimedia Overview," begins some nuts and bolts about multimedia with a review of the kinds of media available on the WWW. Chapter 4, "Web-Ready Materials," deals with getting materials ready for the WWW. To make the WWW work for you, you need to have some notion about how communications are transacted. It's almost like learning a programming language in terms of how it works and what it does. Chapters 5 ("Images"), 6 ("Movies; Desktop Television Editing"), and 7 ("Other Media") focus on a few details about images, movies, sound, and several other media.

Chapter 8 ("Encouraging Web-Based Discussion") turns the focus back to instruction. It deals with strategies for supporting student–student and student–teacher discussion using the WWW. When I dug into the related literature and looked critically around me on my campus at what was going on, I was surprised at the success teachers have had in using the WWW to stimulate and support student discussion. In an age where one might guess that the first teachers using the Web would be scientists and mathematicians exchanging highly technical information with students, one finds, instead, scientists and mathematicians generating student discussion about the technical information.

Chapter 9 ("Interactive Strategies; Forms") is more of what you might expect of technical information being taught on the Web. It focuses on having students respond to specific, sometimes technical questions in a variety of ways. If there is a unique take-away lesson from Chapter 9, it is that quick and dirty e-mail may be the fastest and easiest way for you to start putting useful interactive Web-based responding mechanisms into your students' hands. Meanwhile, the chapter is full of examples — from simple to complex.

When I moved from chemistry to curriculum and instruction, it was mostly the result of many years of concern about the care of the inmates in the asylum. I believe that teachers do matter. Ms. Le Wand, Ms. Leshinsky, Mr. Miller, Mr. Tucker, Dr. Joe Gettler, Dr. John Ricci, Dr. Charlie Dawson, and Dr. Gilbert Stork were darned good teachers for me, and they shaped my life in many ways. Frankly, I can't imagine much learning without teachers. But, it is clear as a bell to me that we are going to be asked to teach students using electronic leveraging systems. My preparation for this book has convinced me that this is not necessarily a bad idea for many students. Some students, however, will be lost and others nearly lost from the gitgo. I think we can try to help those who are nearly lost by taking advantage of information developed over the last 20 years in an area known as self-regulation — strategies for developing the will and the skill to learn. That is what Chapter 10 ("Promotion of Self-Regulated Learning") is all about. When I finished the book, I was disappointed that this chapter was short and picture free. I hope that enormous amounts of good research are performed such that, in a later edition of this book, Chapter 10 will grow and improve more than any of the others.

Chapter 11 ("Creating and Managing Web Sites") deals with setting up Web sites. This is a very simple task.

Bandwidth and security will limit the WWW in many ways. Chapter 12 ("Weblets, CD-ROMs") offers two solutions to the problem. One is to create a subset of the WWW (a counterintuitive move considering what the Web is and what it does), and the other is to create CD-ROMs to hold materials, especially movies and large media files. With ROMs I seek to deliver instruction at the learner's machine rather than over a network. Chapter 13 ("Security Issues; Intranets; Courses for Credit") deals with strategies for security, intranets (networks walled off from the WWW), and some issues related to offering Web-based courses.

Chapter 14 ("Lecturing; Multimedia Classrooms") speaks to lecturing and multimedia classrooms. My view is that converting all of your course materials to WWW formats just with the intent of lecturing is smart. You can have the full multimedia power of the WWW in your classroom. Being able to lecture entirely from Netscape *Navigator* would be a big improvement over the strategies I've needed to use in years past. There also is some information about multimedia classrooms in this chapter for those interested in developing such rooms for lecturing. Having converted your materials, you also place yourself in a near-ready position to provide direct Web-based student access to those same lecture materials.

That's *Web-Teaching*. I hope you find it useful, interesting, and helpful as you think through the many issues concerned with Web-teaching, be that in a small classroom or throughout the entire electronic world.

# ACKNOWLEDGMENTS

Helen Brooks has been my personal and professional partner for 35 years. She knows as much about creating multimedia materials for teachers as anyone else I know. I appreciate not only the suggestions she provided for the book, but her patience throughout the long writing process.

Frank Collea and Karen Cohen are the folks who got this project started. Frank is one of the most thoughtful innovators in science education today. Karen, editor of the *Journal of Science Education and Technology*, served as a concept editor for this project, and coined the title term, *Web-teaching*.

David Fowler, my colleague, is the most futuristic academician I know. Not only did he read an early manuscript and make many helpful suggestions, but he is always pointing me toward the future.

Gregg Schraw opened my eyes to the possibilities for teaching self-regulation. This may prove to be the most important task for all teachers during the next decade or two.

Ken Jensen, manager of the Instructional Design Center at the University of Nebraska, has been one of my most important teachers. Ken's work is remarkable; he always seeks to keep our production facilities at the forefront.

Robert Fuller, an internationally known physics teacher, has pioneered in many technology projects. Without his presence on my campus, I suspect that much less would be accomplished in physics education.

Scott Grabinger of the University of Colorado at Denver was the first person to introduce me to the serious literature of instructional technology.

Charles Ansorge, Steve Ernst, David Hibler, John Orr, and Alan Steckelberg are faculty colleagues who use the Internet and/or WWW for instruction. I've learned a great deal from all of these people. Charles was the first faculty member on my campus to make serious use of the Internet for instruction. Several years ago he ran much of his course material from a gopher site. Steve was among the first faculty to create home pages for courses. The work of David, John, and Alan is mentioned in the book.

John Gelder of Oklahoma State University has been developing outstanding computer-based instructional materials since the late 1970s. His recent work with courses delivered by satellite, coupled with the excellent materials he developed for that course, has given me very different ways of looking at successful instruction.

Lynne Herr is a remarkably critical reader with deep insights about how students learn. She also is one of the best — perhaps *the* best teacher of teachers in use of the Internet in this region. Lynne made an extensive review of the draft manuscript.

Amjad Abuloum is an innovative designer of JavaScripted-pages and interactive-cgis. He brings new intensity to the adjective *enthusiastic*.

Jeff Buell is a remarkably creative materials developer. A whiz with Macromedia *Director*, a consummate problem solver, and a repository for the trivial facts that make powerful development possible, he is one of the most valuable consultants a developer could have for nearly any media project.

Alan Runge maintained all of our multimedia classrooms for some time, and provided substantial help related to discussion in Chapter 14 on developing classrooms.

Susan Gay is a geography teacher who really understands how to make technology work for teachers. Conversations with her always are enlightening. Susan also made an extensive review of the manuscript.

Harry Pence of SUNY Oneonta and Phil Krebs of Sacred Heart University are chemistry teachers who make extensive use of multimedia in their classrooms. Both read early drafts of the manuscript and provided very useful insights.

John Beck is a cinematographer with whom I've worked on several videodisk projects over the last decade. John taught me how to see.

John Ansorge has a deep understanding of desktop television, and he taught me a great deal about computer-driven TV.

Michael Abraham, Thomas Greenbowe, Phil Johnson, and Vickie Williamson provided some very challenging discussion about learning theory — all four of these persons are extremely competent instructional designers.

Robert Egbert provides me with broad-based advice and references on nearly all instructional issues.

Dave Bentz and Brent Sallee provided numerous suggestions about Web techniques. Both have a fifth sense for sniffing out useful tools for Webmasters on the WWW.

Mimi Wickless has shared her terrific sense of how to engage both middle school kids and preservice teachers in science and technology activities.

David Bahr and Mary Curioli of Plenum Publishing edited the manuscript, and provided numerous helpful suggestions and comments.

# CONTENTS

# Web-Teaching

## A Guide to Designing Interactive
## Teaching for the World Wide Web

# CHAPTER 1

# INTRODUCTION

*Web-Teaching*\*[1] is a book about teaching, especially interactive teaching, using the **World Wide Web**\* (WWW) as a communications medium.

In 1989, the CERN High Energy Physics Lab proposed developing a system that would permit ready access to many kinds of computer information and link information together. The result was the *World Wide Web* proposal, the key features of which are a single interface and hyperlinks. Although reference to it appears in the title of this book, the WWW obviously is new.

> World Wide Web: The newest and most ambitious of the special Internet services. World Wide Web browsers can display styled text and graphics. Often abbreviated WWW.
>
> Engst, 1995, Glossary; **URL**\* D

The Web brings a couple of very important features to the Internet. First, unlike **Gopher**\* or anything else, it provides access to full fonts, sizes, and styles for text, and can include images on screen with no special treatment. Sounds and movies are also possible, though often too large for many people to download and view. Second, the Web provides true hypertextual links between documents anywhere on the Web, not just on a single machine. For those unfamiliar with hypertext, it's a powerful concept that enables you to navigate flexibly through linked pieces of information. If you read a paragraph with a link promising more information about the topic, say results from the last Olympic Games, simply click on the link, and you'll see the results. It really is that simple, and the World Wide Web enjoys the highest profile of any of the Internet services.

---

[1] The first time a term found in the glossary appears in the text, it appears in bold type marked with an asterisk.

There are more machines whose names start with WWW than anything else now, and the Web is in second place and rapidly catching up with FTP in terms of the amount of data transferred.

Engst, 1995, p. 36; URL D

A minimalist description of the WWW is that it is a new way of publishing, an alternative to books and journals. If that is all that it is — and I think it is much more than that — it ought to have drastic impact on teaching around the world. Many great ideas in life fall asunder for lack of enthusiasm or implementation. The WWW engendered enthusiasm among Internet users, but implementation was weak until the *Mosaic* software package emerged. While this program showed signs of hope, the real thrust for the WWW came with the release of *Netscape Navigator* software.

**The World Wide Web is changing both
what we teach and how we teach it.**

## A CONTEMPORARY EXAMPLE

Perhaps the best way to indicate to a reader what the possibilities are for using the WWW in instruction is to provide an excellent example of current practice. Barrie and Presti [1996; URL AF; Figure 1.1] describe their use of the Web in an upper-division neurobiology course at the University of California at Berkeley. **Clicking\*** in any of the 12 areas of Figure 1.1 brings about rather different results. A few are protected (grades, student **e-mail\*** addresses). There is an *enormous* amount of accessible content. Students discuss questions (news group). Students post term papers, and receive comments from peers. The quality of the posted student work I examined at this site was very high.

Presently, many teachers have **Web sites\*** like this. New ones spring up daily.

## GOALS OF THIS GUIDE

*Web-Teaching* is the book you go to when you are thinking about redesigning your instruction for electronic delivery, especially when using the World Wide Web. *Web-Teaching* has two thrusts: descriptions of what is possible on the Web, and identification of instructional strategies that are likely to be effective. The first is quite concrete. For example, *modest use of the WWW will permit you to "can" your lectures for delivery during a modified classroom session,* and to provide readily some student support materials that once were difficult to deliver. Therefore, it is important for you to have some idea about what is possible. This is a dynamic target; it is unlikely that the technology available at the moment this book goes to press will be the same as that avail-

Figure 1.1.    Screen capture from course site of neurobiology class at UC-Berkeley.

able when it sells in printed form just weeks later.    The half-life of the information provided for much of the book's contents is better measured in units of months rather than years.    Most of the chemistry content in my 1958 college general chemistry book still remains correct and up-to-date.    Essentially none of the computer-related material presented in this book *existed* in 1958.    In fact, much of it is less than 2 years old!

It is my hope that the second goal, *to get teachers to favor one kind of instructional strategy over another*, will have greater staying power.    The growth in our understanding of the learning process over the past two decades has been enormous.    One can speak with considerable confidence about many biological aspects of human memory [for example, see Pressley and McCormick, 1995, Chapter 6].    Pacesetters even have dared to suggest biological bases for how humans think [Crick, 1994].    The links between this theoretical base and classroom practice are very weak, however.

Education is a field notorious for whimsy, and most innovations are not sustained very long [Ellis and Fouts, 1993].    The notion of having students actively engaged while learning (as opposed to passively listening or reading) is emerging with substantial research support [Ellis and Fouts, 1993].    Because the WWW is a communications medium in which passivity is very possible, those seeking to use this medium must become aware of strategies for interactivity. For this reason, Chapters 8–10 address the development of interactive learning, and mean the most to me.    I hope these work well for many teachers.

Chapter 2 reviews relevant dimensions of learning theory.    Chapters 3–7 are intended to provide an overview of what is possible on the WWW.    These chapters are intended especially for those readers starting out without much knowledge about technology beyond word processing and e-mail.    Chapters 11– 13 focus on some management issues related to Web sites.    Chapter 14 discusses ways to use WWW software to create **multimedia\*** lectures for in-class use, and provides suggestions about setting up multimedia rooms.


## THE INTENDED AUDIENCE

The primary audience for *Web-Teaching* includes teachers and trainers in high school, college, graduate school, in-service education, professional development, adult education, and industry. They can use the WWW to accomplish teaching. They might just as easily, and possibly more effectively, create a secured **intranet\*** within a school or company and use this to link to students or employees over space and time.

Hopefully the suggestions about teaching in *Web-Teaching* are both valid and applicable to nearly all teachers and trainers, as well as to nearly all teaching and training situations. This is not just a book about instruction, however; it is a book about *technology and instruction*. Therefore, the audience is likely to be largely teachers and trainers with particular bents and biases toward technology.

If you are asking yourself "Why write a book instead of using the WWW?" then you are an excellent candidate for reading *Web-Teaching*. If you regularly use e-mail and a word processor, and occasionally surf the net, you're also a strong candidate. Books are not likely to disappear anytime soon. Book production and sales were much higher after the introduction of television than before. Paper use increased after the development of computers.

If you rarely use e-mail, if you can't use a computer effectively, or if you have most of your busywork handled by a secretarial assistant, then you are likely to find *Web-Teaching* amusing, intimidating, or both. If you are hesitating about using the WWW because you can't see yourself as running a **server\***, don't let that stop you. If someone else runs your server, *Web-Teaching* will offer explicit suggestions enabling you to communicate your needs to that person. In fact, all you need to do is get a copy of *Web-Teaching* for that person. Most of all, I can't stress enough how easy it is to create your own Web server.

Finally, if you want to introduce multimedia into your classroom but don't want to bother with any aspects of the WWW at this time, *Web-Teaching* still has valid suggestions to assist you. You might also examine *The Electronic Classroom* [Boschmann, 1995].


## TASKS AND THE NEW TECHNOLOGIES; CURRICULA

If learning miracles occur, they seem to be quite rare. Digital tools don't make learning tasks easier or make learning burdens go away. The tools *do* change, in a very fundamental way, the nature of the task. Norman [1991] calls such tools *cognitive artifacts\** — creations that change the nature of the task and, therefore, the core skills required for success. In my view, much of curriculum reform can and should be viewed in terms of the impact of a seemingly endless stream of cognitive artifacts. Too often, polar terms such as *good/bad* or *fundamental/applied* cloud curriculum development issues. In an era when, in task after task, the carbon cognition of the human brain is being supplanted by the silicon cognition of a desktop computer, we should expect curriculum development to be an immense struggle.

As tools emerge, and tasks change, curriculum reform follows. For example, there has been substantial discussion of the "role of technology" in algebra teaching [Waits and Demana, 1992; Dugdale *et al.*, 1995]. Consider the role of exact numbers in the curriculum before graphing calculators. In those circumstances, the exact number

$$\frac{1+\sqrt{5}}{3}$$

would play a big role. Today this is less important, and graphing becomes more important — because the kinds of questions one can ask and the understandings one can arrive at are deeper. So, pencil and paper or a simple electronic calculator enable dealing with both the exact number and the graph. Although possible, the graph is very tedious to create and interpret using paper, even when the calculations are performed point by point using an electronic calculator. The graphing calculator tool and the computer tool both change that task and thereby cause a reevaluation of the task — increasing the importance of graphing (Figure 1.2).

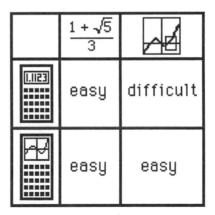

Figure 1.2. With both ordinary and graphing calculators, calculations of exact numbers are easy and straightforward. Although possible with an ordinary calculator, a graphing calculator makes analysis of graphical functions much easier. Therefore, knowledge of graphing becomes more valuable, and graphical analysis is more likely to be applied in practical situations, such as with chemistry "titration" curves.

When teaching **spreadsheets\***, I rarely miss a chance to show what happens to the function *cx(1-x)* when the result from one calculation is cycled back into the succeeding calculation. Depending on the value of $c$ and the initial value of $x$, the result after many iterations may be a constant, or become bistable, or even become chaotic. The spreadsheet performs simple arithmetic (multiplication, subtraction). However, the tedium of the arithmetic is enormous. Virtually no one of my generation, as students, either studied this or was aware of this result. Demonstration of the phenomenon using a spreadsheet takes seconds — and permits vastly different approaches to certain real-world problems. Now that the spreadsheet tool is available, something rarely touched on 15 years ago becomes routine — because the tool made the task so much easier (Figure 1.3).

| | A | B | C | D | E |
|---|---|---|---|---|---|
| **1** | 0.8000 | 1.5000 | 3.1000 | 3.5000 | 3.9000 |
| **2** | 0.1000 | 0.1000 | 0.1000 | 0.1000 | 0.1000 |
| **3** | 0.0720 | 0.1350 | 0.2790 | 0.3150 | 0.3510 |
| **4** | 0.0535 | 0.1752 | 0.6236 | 0.7552 | 0.8884 |
| **5** | 0.0405 | 0.2167 | 0.7276 | 0.6470 | 0.3866 |
| **6** | 0.0311 | 0.2546 | 0.6143 | 0.7993 | 0.9249 |
| **192** | 0.0000 | 0.3333 | 0.5580 | 0.8750 | 0.7328 |
| **193** | 0.0000 | 0.3333 | 0.7646 | 0.3828 | 0.7636 |
| **194** | 0.0000 | 0.3333 | 0.5580 | 0.8269 | 0.7041 |
| **195** | 0.0000 | 0.3333 | 0.7646 | 0.5009 | 0.8125 |
| **196** | 0.0000 | 0.3333 | 0.5580 | 0.8750 | 0.5940 |
| **197** | 0.0000 | 0.3333 | 0.7646 | 0.3828 | 0.9405 |
| **198** | 0.0000 | 0.3333 | 0.5580 | 0.8269 | 0.2182 |

Figure 1.3. Spreadsheet for the function $cx(1-x)$ where the result of one calculation is used for the value of x in the next calculation. The constant, $c$, is found in Row 1. Columns A through E are for values of $c = 0.8, 1.5, 3.1, 3.5,$ and $3.9$, respectively. All initial values of $x$ are set to 0.1000 (Row 2). Note that the outcomes vary, with stable results for A and B, a bistable result for C, a tetrastable result for D, and a chaotic result for E. Though these results may be obtained by hand or with an electronic calculator, the 198 iterations of each formula are handled very quickly and simply using a spreadsheet (Microsoft *Excel*).

Evidence about tool use has emerged in the teaching of mathematics. Graphing calculators and symbolic algebra programs have come to be studied first. Both of these exemplify the kinds of digital tools scientists have available today. While fears about the loss of core skills linger, objective studies support the notion that, when students use these tools extensively and nearly exclusively (as opposed to mixed calculator and conventional pencil and paper, for example), there are substantial learning gains [Pressley and McCormick, 1995, p. 434]. For example, students using graphing calculators have deeper and more extensive understandings of the concept of a function than those using pencil and pa per. A few studies support the same kinds of gains for symbolic mathematics programs [Cooley, 1995; Park, 1993; Porzio, 1994].

Graphing calculators can include what amount to small spreadsheets. Chemists often use spreadsheets to calculate "titration" curves, and compare the calculated curves with experimental results. Graphing calculators, together with calculator-based laboratories (CBLs), can display experimental data together with calculated curves. Figure 1.4 shows a calculated titration curve obtained with a TI-83 graphing calculator; the same device can be used for experiments. Remarkable advances like this have become commonplace over the last 30 years. In my experience, this sort of technology is leading to strong collaborations between chemistry and mathematics teachers at the secondary level, something rare just a few years ago.

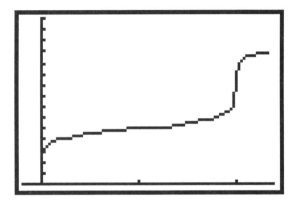

Figure 1.4. Theoretical curve for "titration" of weak acid using strong base graphed using a TI-83 calculator. It is not unusual for students to own calculators with this level of calculating power, nor is it unusual that they understand rather deeply how to use them.

The research results on graphing calculators and symbolic mathematics programs are not surprising. To use the new tools one must understand the concepts in a deep way. You can't just bluff your way through or get by as the result of demonstrating simple calculating skills. My generation was asked to perform on examinations involving demonstrations of skills such as differentiating a function or solving a differential equation. Most of the skill aspect of these tasks is subsumed by computers or calculators. Planning solutions to problems is most of what remains for the professional who uses one of these new tools. For both the professional and the student, many more problems can be worked. As a result, the kinds of experiences a student can have today are *much* broader than when I was a student. Thirty years ago, asking to have many deep and complex problems solved at the levels typically expected in current courses would have constituted cruel and unusual punishment — because of the massive amount of busywork involved.

My sense is that powerful technologies exacerbate core differences in abilities: technology is not an equalizer. Relative professional success is likely to be reflected in who best uses the new tools. There seems to be little hope for the professional futures of those persons who cannot use these tools at all. Those whose lives depended on doing tedious, algorithmic, routine work find greater challenges when seeking employment than just 10 or 15 years ago.

When new technologies become the focus of instruction, substantial learning gains *may* result! These gains are by no means automatic. Lecturers using these tools may feel much better about their classes, and their students may rate those classes more highly than conventional classes, but large learning gains are not inevitable [Cassanova, 1996]. Gains seem to appear mostly when the students themselves use the tools extensively [Cooley, 1995; Park, 1993; Porzio, 1994].

## THE WRITING

No one knows for sure how the WWW will ultimately be used in teaching. As Engst noted in his book, the WWW is both a new and mushrooming phenomenon [Engst, 1995]. Although the WWW has been around for some time, it received little world attention until *Mosaic* software was developed. The WWW has grown extremely rapidly since the first release of *Netscape Navigator*. Throughout my career as a teacher and education researcher, I've used multimedia. My experience gives me some sense of how multimedia on the Web might evolve. My view is that no author can write authoritatively and in a detached manner about how the changes will take place. Multimedia on the Web is as much a "moving target" as any.

Therefore, I decided to write much of *Web-Teaching* using the first person singular. The views expressed are mostly my own. Especially with respect to projections of matters technological, my views are mostly hunches based on experience. The era of the WWW has just begun. Both the scope and duration of this innovation remain to be determined.

I now teach in graduate programs in education at the University of Nebraska. Most faculty who teach similar courses do not come from a content background. My background in chemistry is such that, as I advocate a particular strategy or approach, I'm likely to follow it with a chemistry example or two.

Innovators often overestimate the rate of change but underestimate the extent of change from innovation [Drucker, 1977]. Certainly I spent much of my midcareer, like many others, using modern technology to implement the chemistry curriculum of the 1970s. I didn't properly appreciate the extent that the technologies would change the way chemistry is done and, therefore, change the curriculum. By the same token, it certainly is time for a book about Web-teaching. You can go to the WWW and seek information, but you may be overwhelmed by what is there for you. My goal is to sort through issues and focus your attention. That's why this information appears in a book rather than as part of a Web site.

It often is said that today's students are visual learners. I know too much about genetics to believe in the possible evolution of the typical student mind in less than a decade. Any change in minds will require either hundreds of generations or some crisis in the gene pool. I think it is much easier to defend the position that students read less and, therefore, are different as a result of being less-skilled readers. One early, anecdotal report suggested that student reading skills are improving as a result of surfing the Web. This notion makes sense to me. When kids play with most electronic games, reading is not required extensively. There is no way to navigate the WWW if you can't read.

## SELF-REGULATION

Persons who learn effectively without much teaching or imposed structure usually are good **self-regulators\***. This means that they create for themselves the kind of learning environments that are created by effective teachers. My sense is that WWW-based instruction can be used to enhance students' abilities in the area of self-regulation. Chapter 10 is devoted to suggestions about reaching this goal.

I suspect that the WWW is an ideal medium for good self-regulators, but that it will turn out to be a deadly place for poor self-regulators. This hypothesis may be worthy of experimentation.

## REFERENCES — URLS

In preparing references for *Web-Teaching*, a serious problem was encountered. Users of the WWW are familiar with the acronym URL (uniform resource locator). The Web is an excellent source of information. However, unlike a text where a print copy preserves information that may be stored in a library facility, the electronic information obtained from a URL can be volatile. The server can go off-line and/or someone can remove, or just rename or relocate, the files.

In *Web-Teaching*, references to URLs are presented with a label, the URL itself, and the title of the page that appears for that URL. Occasionally other remarks may be added. URLs are listed on pp. 203-205.

The last thing done before *Web-Teaching* went to press was to check that all of the URLs mentioned in the book were still active.

# CHAPTER 2

# RESEARCH ON TEACHING; WEB ISSUES

Using the WWW for teaching is new. There is no solid research base to consult for guidance. On the other hand, there are things learned from teaching in other venues that are likely to help or guide those interested in using the Web for instruction. This chapter draws on research results in making suggestions about creating learning environments.

## TEACHERS AND FACE VALIDITY

A proposition has *face validity* when it seems reasonable, rational, and appropriate just for what it is without any need for further justification or research. Face validity is akin to "horse sense." A very good teacher of mine once said that horse sense was very good, especially when you're a horse.

> Face validity is concerned with the degree to which a test *appears* to measure what it purports to measure, whereas the other forms of test validity we have described *provide evidence* that the test measures what it purports to measure. ...
> ... Persons tested with such measures often reject the results or refuse to cooperate because they cannot perceive any relationship between the test and the maladjustment. Thus, face validity can be an important consideration in selecting tests for use in situations where subject acceptance is essential. However, a test can appear to be valid when evidence for the other kinds of test validity indicates it is not. Therefore, let us emphasize again that face validity can only supplement information about predictive, concurrent, construct, or content validity of a test and can *never take the place of such information.*
> Borg and Gall, 1989, pp. 256-257

There are several areas where face validity comes into conflict with research results in ways that affect what teachers do.

**Four notions related to teaching that have face validity but are *not* well supported by research are:**

- **The more teachers can show them about learning something, the more students will learn.**

- **Multimedia affords an inherently better way to teach.**

- **Students differ in learning style. The more the teacher knows about a learner's style, the better she or he can teach that person.**

- **The quality of face-to-face discussions is higher than that of electronically conducted discussions.**

## A SUMMARY OF RESEARCH POSITIONS

Teachers can design creative instructional materials for WWW-based instruction of two types. One type requires **active learning\***; the other presents the materials in a way that an excellent lecturer might present them. *Teachers who demand active learning are likely to bring about substantially greater learning success than those who do not.* My advice is to keep the learners' brains running in high gear whenever possible; make learners work; keep learners active.

The WWW is an attractive delivery system for multimedia, and many teachers believe that replacing text with pictures and other media will bring about much better student learning. Rarely is this intuition supported by research. My advice in this area is simple: pick the Web medium you think best suited for covering a particular topic and use it. Don't ascribe special teaching power to that medium.

If we could measure a learner's style or type and then teach to it, learning might improve. Perhaps someday this will be possible. Today such an outcome is not supported by research. So, my advice is to not be deeply concerned about anything except, perhaps, the expected text reading level and experiential background of your learners. If you feel strongly that I dismiss this issue too readily, see the rather optimistic and personal discussion of this issue offered by Sternberg [1994]. (Frankly, I suspect that what Sternberg did was introduce active learning strategies into his teaching. The "style" he describes himself as preferring is, one for one, my style. The introductory psychology teacher Sternberg mentions probably had that style, too.)

Early results on **Internet\***-based learning suggest that discussion can be very effective when held over the WWW with learners who are adults. Since discussion strategies are easily implemented and may give the best approach to active learning, give this format early and serious consideration in your planning processes.

## ACTIVE LEARNING; INTERACTIVE TEACHING

In any "school" model for changing someone's intellectual skills, abilities, or knowledge, two different roles typically are described: the student and the teacher. The student or learner is the person whose behavior is targeted for change. Too often teachers forget that it is possible to have learning *without* teachers. The best learners seem to be able to teach themselves. For the best learners, much teaching is informal — often based on responses to questions they formulate and ask of their "teachers." For the best learners, teachers might be described as resource persons. It also should be noted that, for most teachers, most students are not well described by the term *best learners*.

**teach** (*v*)

(tr)

1. To impart knowledge or skill to: teaches children.
2. To provide knowledge of; instruct in: teaches French.
3. To condition to a certain action or frame of mind: teaching youngsters to be self-reliant.
4. To cause to learn by example or experience: an accident that taught me a valuable lesson.
5. To advocate or preach: teaches racial and religious tolerance.
6. To carry on instruction on a regular basis in: taught high school for many years.

—*intr.*

To give instruction, especially as an occupation.

Synonyms:   teach, instruct, educate, train, school, discipline, drill. These verbs mean to impart knowledge or skill.   Teach is the most widely applicable: teaching a child the alphabet; teaches political science. "We shouldn't teach great books; we should teach a love of reading" (B.F. Skinner). Instruct usually suggests methodical teaching:   A graduate student instructed the freshmen in the rudiments of music theory. Educate often implies formal instruction but especially stresses the development of innate capacities that leads to wide cultivation:   "All educated Americans, first or last, go to Europe" (Ralph Waldo Emerson). Train suggests concentration on particular skills intended to fit a person for a desired role:   The young woman attends vocational school, where she is being trained as a computer technician. School often implies an arduous learning process:   The violinist had been schooled to practice slowly to assure accurate intonation.   Discipline usually refers to the teaching of control, especially self-control: The writer has disciplined himself to work between breakfast and lunch every day. Drill implies rigorous instruction or training, often by repetition of a routine: The French instructor drilled the students in irregular verbs.

### learn                                                          (*v*)
(tr)
1. To gain knowledge, comprehension, or mastery of through experience or study.
2. To fix in the mind or memory; memorize: learned the speech in a few hours.
3.a. To acquire experience of or an ability or a skill in: learn tolerance; learned how to whistle. b. To become aware: learned that it was best not to argue.
4. To become informed of; find out. ...

*—intr.*
To gain knowledge, information, comprehension, or skill: learns quickly; learned about computers; learned of the job through friends.

### student (n)
1. One who attends a school, college, or university.
2a. One who makes a study of something. b. An attentive observer: a student of world affairs.

American Heritage Talking Dictionary CD-ROM<br>
SoftKey International, Inc.<br>
Cambridge, MA 02139

It is not surprising that many teachers favor learning materials that are teacher centered. After all, the teacher knows the material but the students don't. The teacher's job is to get the material across to the students. This view has face validity in the school model. It is well accepted by most students, school administrators, teachers, and parents, and well put forth in the definition of the word *student*. Again, most research does not usually support the teacher-centered model as a preferred model, especially when pitted against active learning models.

Curriculum materials that force students to respond, to make choices, to perform, to organize, to think deeply about the material, and so forth have better outcomes, generally, than ones in which they just read or listen. The former behaviors often are labeled under the heading of *active learning*, and much research indicates that active learning is more effective than passive learning. With curriculum materials that encourage active learning, the teacher often is silent. As a psychometric construct, active learning leaves much to be desired, however.

Typically, active learning is defined in contrast to the worst of traditional teaching in which teachers actively present information and students passively receive it. This definition says more about what active learning is not than about what it is. And since we know of no generally agreed upon definition of active learning ...

Meyers and Jones, 1993, p. 19

in *Promoting Active Learning*

The term *active learning* echoes in the halls of curriculum and instruction departments like mine but usually remains absent from works on teaching written by members of educational psychology departments. If one looks at materials written by learning experts, this topic usually doesn't seem to appear in either the tables of contents or the indexes. By comparison, Pressley and McCormick, very effective writers in terms of suggesting explicit approaches to improving teaching, offer a summary of strategies for improving instruction.

Because this chapter presented a mixture of interventions that definitely work to improve student learning, thinking, and performance; others that have small or inconsistent effects at best; and still others that are untested for the most part, we summarize in the table below what was covered in this chapter regarding documented efficacy with respect to stimulating student achievement. ...

**Certain Effects**

Attending school, especially "effective" orderly schools
Academically oriented, engaging classrooms
Head Start and early intervention programs
One-on-one tutoring, including as it occurs in programs such as Success for All and after school, as in the *Juku* system
Teacher questioning
Wait time during teacher questioning
Student questioning
Differential teacher reactions to students on basis of ability
Parental involvement in schooling
Volunteer tutors in classrooms
Peer tutoring
Smaller classes
Mastery learning
Homework, especially after the elementary-school years
Viewing educational television
Higher education

College major
Some college courses

### Small, Uncertain, Negative, or Not Tested Satisfactorily
Teacher expectancies (mixed evidence)
Ability grouping and tracking (negative)
Sex-segregated classrooms (small)
Retention of students in a grade (negative)
Short-term summer school programs (small)
Extracurricular activities (uncertain)
After-school work (negative)
Viewing entertainment television (negative)
Thinking skills programs (not tested sufficiently)
Mentors in college (not tested sufficiently)

from *Advanced Educational Psychology for Educators, Researchers, and Policymakers* by Michael Pressley with Christine B. McCormick. Copyright © 1995 by Michael Pressley and Christine B. McCormick. Reprinted by permission of Addison-Wesley Educational Publishers, Inc.

The reason to advocate active learning strategies is that, when well developed, the effects can be large — quite large. Because of the rather large potential for big gains, three chapters of *Web-Teaching* have been devoted to active learning strategies. *Just clicking around the Web (surfing) is not an especially effective learning strategy, in my view.* Purposeless surfing of the WWW is not likely to bring about learning gains. Indeed, purposeful surfing may be very limited in its impact.

Several studies have been reported in which graphing calculators or powerful software (*Mathematica, Maple*, molecular structure software) is incorporated into teaching. College-level students using graphing calculators came to understand the concept of function substantially better than did students in traditionally taught control classes [Pressley and McCormick, 1995, p. 434]. When the software is demonstrated in lecture classes, learning gains are small or nonexistent [Klein, 1993]. In chemistry, students sometimes lost ground in classes with technology-based software presentations but little or no learner practice with feedback [Cassanova and Cassanova,1991; Cassanova, 1996]. When the technology is put in the students' hands, and the instruction modified to include activities that illustrate the power of the software, learning gains often are substantial [Cooley, 1995; Park, 1993; Porzio, 1994]. Again, when teaching newer technologies (calculators, software), strategies for active learning consistently seem to give better results.

"Real-world" activities have proven to be the best kinds of experiences in many situations. They force active learning, and they provide realistic environments that have a way of nurturing motivation. Real-world activities are limited and still relatively unusual as far as being included within routine school-based instruction. Teachers struggle to create effective active learning environments in classrooms and laboratories. It *remains* a challenge to see how the principles of active learning can be incorporated into Web-based learning. There are exciting possibilities: the instructional delivery system is at the same time the world-wide scientific communication system. Clever teachers already have found ways to involve students. Scientists have found ways to recruit students as observers — as in the monarch butterfly project [URL A, Figure 2.1].

Figure 2.1. Screen capture from the home page of the Monarch Butterfly Watch, a national WWW-connected project.

Certainly active learning was not a part of the early days of instructional television, where students watched passively, often gazing at a screen of a professorial **talking face\*** taped during a traditional lecture class. There is no assurance that Web-based materials need engender active learning. Poorly designed materials can be a few clicks beyond early educational TV.

## MULTIMEDIA; DEVELOPING A PERSPECTIVE

The World Wide Web is a communications system far broader than an electronic text with color pictures: it is rather a **comprehensive multimedia delivery system\***.

**mul•ti•me•di•a,** *pl.n.* (used with a sing. verb).
1. The combined use of several media, such as movies, slides, music, and lighting, especially for the purpose of education or entertainment.
2. The use of several mass media, such as television, radio, and print, especially for the purpose of advertising or publicity. Also called mixed media.

**mul•ti•me•di•a,** *attributive n.*
Often used to modify another noun: a multimedia presentation; a multimedia advertising campaign
American Heritage Talking Dictionary CD-ROM
SoftKey International, Inc., Cambridge, MA 02139

*Multimedia* is a term whose implications have evolved.  Thirty years ago, when I started teaching, it implied using slides or super-8 movies or TV in teaching.  Today it implies using computers.  Computers deliver text, pictures, **movies\***, **animations\***, molecular structures, sounds, music, and can interact with virtually every sense except taste and smell.  These probably will be developed eventually, too.  Notice that the definition given by a **CD-ROM\*** dictionary (a source that *pronounces* the word *multimedia*) makes no mention of either digitization or computers.  Sellers of the ROM would be the first to tell you that it was a multimedia dictionary and that it was part of the computer age.

The citation on the Internet electronic cataloguing system called *Yahoo* may give a quite different impression of this term:

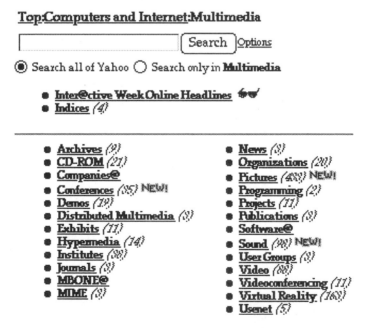

Figure 2.2.  January 1997 screen capture from Computers_and_Internet/Multimedia found at *Yahoo*, the innovative WWW cataloguing and searching system [URL AH].

Multimedia instruction passes the most important test that instructional materials must pass before they are used in classrooms, namely, face validity in the eyes of the teacher. When committed teachers see an excellent multimedia piece developed to teach some aspect of their discipline, usually their eyes widen and broad smiles spread across their faces. They are impressed. That certainly is true of me, and it seems true of most of the chemistry teachers I hang around with. In our time, the potential for creating media to portray scientific phenomena visually and aurally is very great. We are no longer constrained such that the words we utter have students conjuring up images in their minds to fit those words. Indeed, we may even introduce biases far and wide about the nature of scientific phenomena through the teaching images we can create today. Are there research results related to teaching using multimedia? When adjusted to account for differences in active learning components, research studies aimed at studying media often show no significant learning differences [Clark, 1983].

> Research projects comparing media treatments with so-called conventional instruction frequently conclude that there is 'no statistically significant difference' in learning between the media-based and conventional instruction. Does this mean that audiovisual presentations are equivalent to lectures? Not necessarily. It may mean that when certain audiovisual materials are used in the same way as a lecture is used (e.g., for verbal recall of information), the outcomes will be similar when observed over a range of learners.
>
> There needs to be some consideration for such important variables as the presence of a creative instructor in the learning experience. In practice, a teacher does not use audiovisual materials in the same way as print or lecture-type materials. Selection of media to suit a particular learning outcome is of particular importance. Audiovisual presentations can be very powerful—for example, in conveying a historical period's feel, in building empathy for others, or in showing a role model in action.
>
> Heinich *et al.*, 1996, p. 27

In the 1960s, Lumsdaine (1963) and others (e.g., Mielke, 1968) argued that gross comparisons of the influence of different media on learning might not be useful. They implied that media, when viewed as no more than collections of electromechanical devices such as television and movies, were simple delivery instruments and that when everything else was held constant, they would not be found to influence learning directly in and of themselves. And while it has been the case that subsequent research has borne out their suspicion, many researchers continued to search for overall learning benefits from media. But, as has become evident, learning from instruction is a much more complicated process that often involves interactions between specific tasks, particular learner traits, and various components of medium and method. In this mix, the effects of gross, undifferentiated "medium" variables could not be productive. Part of the reason for the continued reliance on media comparisons was that earlier reviewers held the door open to media influences on learning by blaming much of the lack of systematic findings in prior research on poor research design and on a lack of adequate theory.

Clark and Salomon, 1986, p. 465

When asked to read about a topic or to watch a video about the same topic, students learn about the same amount. Furthermore, students often prefer the medium from which they learn the least [Clark, 1982]. This is by no means a closed issue. When one reads the literature, it is very clear that instructional design is what is important. It is completely clear that some media enable certain types of instruction much better than others. Interested readers might look at issues 2 and 3 of *Educational Technology Research and Development*, 1995 [Clark, 1995a, b; Jonassen *et al.*, 1995; Kozma, 1995a, b; Morrison, 1995; Reiser, 1995; Ross, 1995 a, b; Shrock, 1995; Tennyson, 1995]. If your time is limited, read the Tennyson article first.

While transforming some content to a multimedia format may be a "cool" and popular thing to do, it by no means ensures learning gains. As a result of the greatly increased power and lowered costs for creating and delivering multimedia, there is an emerging feeling that teaching can be improved by extensive use of multimedia in large lecture courses. Students favor multimediated instruction over conventional ("chalk and talk") instruction [Ansorge and Wilhite, 1994; Pence, 1993]. Thus far, learning *gains* demonstrated from multimedia instruction have been particularly disappointing. Our ability to portray complex ideas concerning such things as molecular phenomena has been enhanced enormously. Students' performances in mediated lecture courses have not changed much at all. Teachers who make extensive use of multimedia may receive high ratings compared to peers, but their students do not necessarily outperform those of peers [Ansorge and Wilhite, 1994]. (One of my reviewers took pains to point out that "rotten" multimedia instruction is possible, too!)

Don't think for a moment that this is a challenge to the notion that attitude is important. This is an assertion that learning is not *always* related to attitude. Further, I think some teachers take this to mean that "if we make students a bit less happy, they may do better." That's *not* what this means at all! Quite the opposite is true. Let's say you have a course where the content is well defined by a book and some other media materials. You can present the material, or you can engage in activities to motivate the students to work with the material, especially with mastery learning as a goal. All of my experience suggests that you'll get better results if you motivate first, and then cover the material. If you already have strongly motivated students who are good self-regulators, just cover the material.

It is important to set forth these views so that, as you work through *Web-Teaching*, you can keep two kinds of issues straight. On the one hand, we'll be advocating the use of multimedia that capture phenomena and portray them in ways heretofore impossible. That should not be confused with active learning strategies. When push comes to shove, *your time will be better spent developing, implementing, and testing active learning strategies.*

## Multimedia in "Teacher-Proof" Settings

This introduction may have caused you to become a bit confused regarding reports you have read about multimedia. Multimedia has advocates of whom I certainly am one. It is clear that many teachers see the introduction of multimedia alone as a means of improving instruction.

Sometimes multimedia is introduced to solve problems with conventional instruction. My own experience is a good example. I turned to multimedia in 1968 while supervising laboratory instruction in the multisection general chemistry program at a major university. We operated on a model of prelaboratory instruction followed by laboratory work in those days. There were something like 15 different prelaboratory instruction sessions each week. Many of these were "covered" by a tenured faculty person who had been "retired" into that task. Rather than discuss the content, he focused on extraneous material related to hunting and fishing. A major reason for introducing multimedia prelab materials was to make instruction more uniform across sections of the course. The use of multimedia at many large schools has been an attempt to deal with issues related to nonuniform instruction, especially ones created as the result of making extensive use of graduate teaching assistants [Haight, 1978; Enger *et al.*, 1978]. The idea is to try to make instruction "teacher proof."

## Multimedia in Active Learning Systems

Often multimedia is embedded in a system of changes that include drastic changes in the expectations for active learning. There have been many reports by Stanley Smith and his collaborators, especially Loretta Jones, in which chemistry learning systems have been developed that make extensive use of multimedia [Smith and Jones, 1989]. Smith's work in this area began during the 1960s, and is especially noteworthy.

Smith's work should not be used as a means of endorsing multimedia instruction. He nearly always describes *learning systems*, ones that demand active participation on the part of the learner. In order to understand his work, one needs to separate multimedia issues from active learning issues. One can argue that this is a moot point, since there would be no realistic way to try to create a learning system like a Smith system without using multimedia. True enough. But what would be the outcome if the systems Smith describes were used as a lecturer's tool in slick multimedia classes during which the lecturer made the choices and spoke aloud while the students listened? My guess — an educated guess — is that the student evaluations would be good, but that little if any learning gain would be demonstrated.

Pence reports very favorable student responses to multimedia, and implies that learning improvements are likely [Pence, 1993]. His use of multimedia, however, involves brief presentations followed by cooperative learning activities between pairs of students in the class. My sense is that any significant learning gains in this environment are related to the active learning strategy carefully integrated with the multimedia rather than just the multimedia alone.

Designing learning experiments is not an easy matter. Even in the best of circumstances, the instructional multimedia are embedded within an instructional delivery setting, and it is very hard to simply replace one medium with another. Also, many times a system that works extremely well in one setting proves not to "have legs." The **audiotutorial system\*** for teaching introductory botany created by S. N. Posthlewaite was remarkably effective at Purdue. Not everyone who adopted this approach to teaching could make it work to the same degree that Posthlewaite could. I actually watched sessions of that system during a visit to Purdue, and I have a sister-in-law who took the course. That was a wonderful course!

Along similar lines, "Keller Plan" courses flourished during the late 1960s and early 1970s [Keller and Sherman, 1974]. In spite of their success, one almost never hears of a Keller course today. My view is that it took more effort to run Keller courses than either teachers or students were willing to expend for the increased learning.

## Instances of Multimedia Superiority?

> Learning is more correctly attributable to well-orchestrated design
> strategies than to the inherent superiority of various media.
>
> Hannafin and Hooper, 1993, p. 192

There are times when intuition leads a teacher to suspect strongly that a multimedia approach will be superior. This again is a face validity matter. Trying to get students to be able to think of chemical phenomena in atomic and molecular terms seems like an ideal case. In a specific test of one aspect of multimedia learning, Williamson and Abraham [1995] report substantial learning gains when animations and visualizations (created by Gelder [1994]) were used to exemplify phenomena at the atomic–molecular level. The durations of the animations were rather brief, as was the total exposure to them. Using an instrument designed specifically to assess learning in this concept realm, the effect size of the significant impact of using the multimedia was quite large. Just seeing the animations in lecture led to large gains in scores on the measuring instrument; no additional benefit accrued from additional access during computer lab time. However, these gains did not show up on overall course exam scores, individual items, or attitude assessments. This work is cited informally by many chemistry educators as support for the multimedia effort. If a dozen studies like this showed similar results, perhaps the enthusiasm of this support would be justifiable. Abraham and I both are surprised by the large size of the effect given the brief duration of the intervention. To one who holds views that learning is neurologically based, the outcome implies either that the learning is trivial (in conflict with this author's personal sense of face validity on this issue) or that the assessment is somehow trivial and is missing the mark. Abraham points to similarly vexing gains in the area of creativity subsequent to brief interventions [Abraham, 1996].

It is a stretch to try to make sense of the Williamson–Abraham result. In *The Language Instinct*, Steven Pinker [1994] attributes human language to inborn neurological tools — *instinct* being a very appropriate term. A major notion in the book is that nearly all children develop language skills by 36 months that are remarkable in breadth and depth but that are not attributable to exposure. Perhaps what humans have is a remarkable facility for pattern recognition, and speech and the impact of animations are examples of that pattern recognition ability emerging. As a substantive aside during a recent presentation, Chapman reported significant learning improvements in students' ability to comprehend nuclear magnetic resonance spectra as a result of a brief but very concerted and well-planned exposure to a very large series of spectral patterns [Chapman *et al.*, 1996]. Perhaps this also is not an example of trivial learning, but rather a result of especially keen human skill. Another possible explanation is that the animation makes the explanation so much more concrete than abstract as to make it more memorable.

The materials tested by Williamson and Abraham were part of those developed for an AP Chemistry via satellite course. In spite of the quality of the materials and the demonstrable excellence of the teacher, student success rates as judged by AP scores were "average." Although geared toward AP, many students chose not to take the AP test. In other words, when used throughout a well-designed and well-delivered course, evidence of magic from use of the multimedia materials disappeared.

Animations afford excellent means for teachers to convey concepts. When you can buy them off the shelf, an enormous amount of work has been accomplished for you. Without animations a teacher can talk about these concepts at the podium, fumbling with chalk or overhead projector pens to try to convey the relevant concepts. Using Gelder's animations serves the teacher's purpose exceptionally well, that is, to convey to students the concepts of how one might view the atomic and molecular world. *ChemAnimations* [Gelder, 1994], and the *Saunders Interactive General Chemistry* CD-ROM developed by Kotz and Vining [1996, Figure 2.3] are examples of commercial materials that afford chemistry teachers the easiest way to present complex ideas with minimal teacher preparation or media materials. An enormous amount of thinking has already been incorporated into these materials.

Animations also may serve the purpose of presenting data from an entirely different perspective. That is, the animation may not present information so as to answer the traditional questions in a topic, but rather to generate new questions. Students may see patterns in the data as represented by the unconventional animation in such a way as to help them reanalyze the data along new conceptual lines:

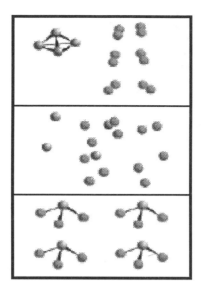

Figure 2.3. Three frames adapted from the elegant animation by Kotz and Vining of the formation of phosphorus trichloride from phosphorus and chlorine.

Computer-assisted geographic visualization is fundamentally different [from earlier formats]. The computer facilitates direct depiction of movement and change, multiple views of the same data, user interaction with maps, realism (through three-dimensional stereo views and other techniques), false realism (through fractal generation of landscapes), and the mixing of maps with other graphics, text, and sound.
MacEachren and Monmonier, 1992, p. 197

## Research in Multimedia

Within a course, if students are expected to learn something, it usually needs to "count" — which nearly always means count toward a course grade. If a component of a course is going to count, then equal access to instructional opportunities seems likely, even in a multisection course. (In science and math courses, equal opportunity for a grade is usually a part of what faculty consider to be fair, and the only variations permitted are those that deal with differences in faculty. "Common" exams, tests in which all students from all sections sit simultaneously, or which are otherwise administered to attempt to ensure near-identical treatment, often are found in multisection science and math courses.) This sense of equity and fair play usually precludes opportunities for traditional controlled experiments in learning. *All* students are either in the control group (what was done last year) or in the treatment group (what we're trying new this year). One recent study from an institution with extremely well-controlled instructional settings showed no difference between traditional and multimedia prelaboratory instruction in terms of student performance [Wessel *et al.*, 1996].

## Commercial Multimedia

There are many commercially available multimedia sources, and these make excellent choices for teachers to use — in the lecture classroom and laboratory. Note, however, that copyright restrictions are likely to impact WWW usage. For this reason, you may want to set up an intranet for which you have negotiated a license. At least you will want to control these media so that student name and password are required before obtaining access.

There are, of course, advantages to using commercial multimedia. Many of the projects supported by the National Science Foundation are commercially available, and licensing these materials for your courses may be the least expensive way for you to acquire quality multimedia materials.

## LEARNING STYLES AND LEARNING

A part of the teacher-oriented high school and college literatures includes many pieces devoted to learning styles. Many teachers speak to differences in learning styles, and urge colleagues to both increase awareness of these differences and account for them in teaching.

If there were a readily identifiable connection between a measurable learning style and success in some teaching strategy, then multimedia instruction could be a boon. Teachers could create alternative instructional strategies, each with appropriate multimedia materials, and then direct students toward that strategy found to be most effective for their style. This notion has high face validity. At first blush, the multimedia-wise teacher sees bright light at the end of the tunnel.

The more serious literature on teaching and learning, such as the excellent text by Pressley and McCormick [1995], rarely mentions learning styles — at least not using the same jargon. Why? Sometimes experiments don't support face validity. Therefore, in the absence of supportable evidence about what to do when designing instruction, I've written this section to discourage you from thinking too much about learning styles as you plan instructional materials for use on the WWW. As noted earlier, the Sternberg [1994] article is of considerable interest.

Consider measures of learner "type" as measured by the popular instrument created by **Myers and Briggs\*** (MB). In the MB scheme, four dimensions of "type" are spoken of: extroversion/introversion (E/I), intuitive/sensory (N/S), thinking/feeling (T/F), and judgmental/perceiving (J/P). One takes a test and the result is reported in terms of a four-letter scale. Mine is INTJ, ENTJ, or XNTJ, depending on how the results are viewed, and when I complete the instrument. Ambivalence on a scale can be represented using the letter X. As for the NTJ part of me, that's pathological! I've probably taken an MB inventory 20 times in my life — I take one every time I teach the material — and the number of times I've chosen a Feeling response (F) over a Thinking response (T) can be counted on the fingers of my hands.

In the MB-like computer program I use, after you respond to 50 items and your type has been determined, you get to read a paragraph about yourself. (Some folks train in the MB system and offer individual counseling interpreting the results. The program I use popped up as **freeware*** several year ago, and its use is frowned on by MB purists.) The paragraphs have a great deal of face validity. A noun often associated with the INTJ type, for example, is *scientist*. That certainly fits me, or at least I like to think that it does. And so it goes. In my classes, where the freeware version of the test is used, my students usually find the descriptive paragraphs very appropriate to how they see themselves. Face validity rises again.

The "soft" literature that suggests how an INTJ might teach an ESFP is largely inferred. When one goes to test the kinds of suggestions that are made, one finds low or no correlation between student learning and type [Pittenger, 1993]. So, there you have it. High face validity in the eyes of the teacher perpetuates a belief system that is not supported by research. Performing this research, by the way, is less difficult than is testing multimedia in an experiential setting. The independent variable can be MB type, and the dependent variable performance in some portion of a course, or some affective assessment about some dimension of the course. The most difficult part can be getting the project approved by a human experiments review panel with their concerns focusing on how the types are assessed and reported.

Other schemes of learning styles often are just as compelling from a face validity perspective, but equally disappointing when the time comes to tie style to teaching practice or learning outcome.

Another style dimension that has something of a research base is that of field dependence/field independence [Witkin *et al.*, 1967]. A field-independent person is better able to disembed a task from its surroundings. Suppose I have a half-filled bottle of soda that I hold vertically by the neck. When asked to draw a sketch about how the soda will look when the bottle is tipped, field-dependent persons tend to draw the surface perpendicular to the walls of the bottle, while field-independent persons draw it parallel to the horizon. This test has large sex

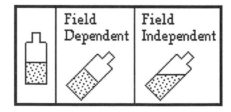

differences, with females tending to be more field dependent. In fact, nearly from the outset significant sex differences in field-dependent/independent performances have been observed [Witkin, 1949]. An instrument often used for this purpose is called the Embedded Figures Test [Witkin *et al.*, 1971]. There are reports that there is an interaction between teacher sex, student sex, field dependence/independence, and final course grades [Bertini, 1986]. Once again, tying a score on this instrument to some instructional strategy has had little payout for teachers, if any. Greenbowe and co-workers very recently have shown a small favorable impact of multimedia instructional materials for female field-dependent students [Greenbowe, 1996].

Finally, there is a counterview about whether teachers should try to tailor instruction to learning styles. In this view, the best outcome for students is to expose them to many kinds of learning experiences regardless of how well these might match each student's style, with the intended goal being to better enable them to learn under a very wide range of situations and circumstances.

## Intelligence

As an extension of style-oriented thinking, there is some hope that one will be able to identify different kinds of aspects of intelligence, and that this may ultimately have some teaching payout [Gardner, 1983; 1993 (paper)]. Currently, however, there is more promise than procedure. For a brief but very readable and middle-of-the-road discussion of intelligence, see Sternberg [1996].

## ARE ELECTRONIC CONVERSATIONS LESS EFFECTIVE?

Face validity supports still another notion, namely, that certain kinds of teaching and interaction require face-to-face meetings and cannot be conducted electronically. Evidence in support of this notion is intuitive rather than based on the literature. Hardly a source one might look to for an objective assessment of the issues related to this question, *Learning Networks* does provide some commentary.

> The traditional face-to-face classroom learning situation is generally assumed to be the best to support learning, with other learning modes perhaps perceived as less effective. There is no evidence to support this assumption. In fact, quite the opposite is true: Online environments facilitate learning outcomes that are equal or superior to those generated in the face-to-face situation (Hiltz 1988a, 1994; Wells 1990).
> Harasim *et al.*, 1995, p 27

Although the three references cited include two by one of *Learning Networks* authors, the entire notion gave me cause for pause. On the one hand, emotional arguments developed over more than three decades of college teaching draw me to the view that the press of the flesh is important and cannot be replaced by some electronic mode. On the other, I really have no basis on which to make this assertion. After all, up until now the kind of computer-moderated communications described have not been possible. Further, my personal experience with Internet-based learning activities for adults causes me to support essentially every conclusion drawn in *Learning Networks* [Liu, 1996].

Several years ago a local collaboration developed to offer Japanese language instruction via satellite. Many reception sites were involved with about 1000 students enrolling each year. When compared with students receiving traditional instruction, distance learners not only performed better on tests but offered more positive course evaluations [Bruning *et al.*, 1993]. That was *not* a WWW study, and there were site instructors involved who were learning the language at the same time as their students, but I still would have predicted higher scores for traditionally enrolled students. The course instructor, Tim Cook, is a terrific teacher! The course evaluator suggested to me that, the better the site instructor was as a student, the better was the learning at that site [Bruning, 1996].

My current view is that a requirement for face-to-face sessions is an open question when teaching adults, a question especially suitable for research. This is a newly held view for me.


## THE WWW AS A DELIVERY MEDIUM

It is clear that the WWW is a low-cost delivery system for multimedia! The Web can be nearly as passive as was television in the early days of instructional TV. If one didn't have to click now and again, it would be every bit as passive. In some ways, "clicking" the remote on a cable TV may be more interactive; one decides after each click whether to stay on the current channel, or to click again.

On the other hand, you can make your WWW-based teaching interactive in an attempt to encourage active learning. The Web's greatest intrinsic power is that it encourages branched, nonlinear instruction. Not only can students jump around among the materials that you have created for them, they also can access materials created by others. Indeed, *they* can create useful materials!

Also, it is quite possible to access misinformation on the WWW, perhaps even more easily than in your daily newspaper. Web-based misinformation is a problem. In McLuhan's sense of the term, everyone is a publisher [McLuhan, 1964]. His reference was to xerographic copiers — which facilitated publication considerably, but nothing to the degree that the WWW has. Where are the Web's editors?

You and your students no longer need to be time bound. A student can log on at essentially any time of the day or night. The student need not be place bound; access can be from wherever there is Internet access.

Imagine yourself having an evening conversation with a student in which you and she are each chatting over a computer linkup. You are both in your respective homes. You see and hear one another. You share a **whiteboard\*** on which both of you can see changes made by the other. This rather personalized interaction, not particularly bound in time or place, is now possible and is becoming commonplace.

The WWW (Internet or intranet) is going to be used for instruction regardless of what teachers think, feel, or do. It will be used even in the absence of demonstrable research support. This delivery method is cheaper! Many costs, particularly costs like hardware and Internet linkup and cleaning and air conditioning, are transferred from the school to the student. You'd better bet that WWW-based instruction will happen.

Should the WWW be used to teach everything? Hardly. I still believe that some of the material I teach requires face-to-face, press-of-the-flesh instruction. Remember, that's an unsupported view, one subject to research. But, because I don't care about your opinion of the mass (in grams) of a sodium atom, I'm completely comfortable handling this content at a distance. Much of what I teach is technical in nature — content that is convergent (i.e., has a single answer). So, without ever leaving my home, I could handle 50 or 100 graduate students effectively in a course that now has just 10 or 20 enrolled students.

## TEACHER AS DESIGNER

Many high school and college teachers have seen themselves as the authors of wonderful lectures. Their goal has been to weave a story about their discipline that evolves logically and engagingly over time. In spite of the criticism that sometimes is placed on the lecture method, that is a proven method of instruction. It has two clear shortcomings. First, not all lecturers are equally gifted. Next, it encourages passive rather than active learning. So, it works well with motivated persons who are good self-regulators.

*Web-Teaching* will suggest ways for you to unabashedly "can" your lectures. In fact, if you really want to, you can deliver canned lectures over the WWW — voice and all! Sometimes that may be perfectly appropriate.

From the outset, it is clear that you easily can plan to spend more time than you actually have in preparing teaching materials. Perhaps you should make a plan to start with a modular or framework approach in which you plan formal stages — first "**Webifying\***" written materials, and then adding **hypertext\*** links, adding multimedia, adding on-line tutoring, adding on-line exams, and so forth.

Quality multimedia is very hard to come by. The more quality you need, the higher is the level of difficulty. Only foolish persons, or those with very large, well-funded teams, should expect to produce substantial amounts of high-quality multimedia courseware in a short time. Nevertheless, it is remarkable how much a teacher with a good notion about the learning difficulties in the content can produce in a reasonable time period using the tools currently available.

Your teaching may be most improved by undertaking a review of how your curriculum encourages active learning and self-regulation. Sometimes a review from the perspective of adding specific materials about self-regulation, both generic information as well as content- and domain-specific information, would be more effective than any "Webification" you might undertake.

## TEACHER AND STUDENT; SERVER AND CLIENT

As the designer of Internet multimedia materials, there is a model that can serve you well. Think of the teachers as the server: what will the server do in response to a client (student) question or request? What should the student see (and hear)? What options should the student have? Should you empower them in a particular instance, or should you insist that they come to you for information and service? You need to decide where to put your programming efforts, if any — on the server side, or the client side. The author's server is shown in Figure 2.4.

Figure 2.4. Server located in the author's office. Arrow points to connection between server and port, the "window to the world."

Most of what you see on the Internet is client-side material. True, branching from one page to another involves returning to the server. But many leaps are within pages. Most **browsers\*** support client-side **"maps\*"** that empower the user to make choices at the client side without returning to the server.

Very interactive teaching requires that students also create and transmit information, ask open-ended questions, and so forth.   In the best of teaching situations, your learners will have browsers that use powerful tools you've created for them to accomplish these tasks.

## THE VOICE OF THE TEACHER

One feature of the WWW is that, given free access, students can range far and wide.  Judah Schwartz has discussed this issue.   In conventional curricular materials, teachers have an excellent idea of where students have been and what they know — at least as far as a particular body of content is concerned.  If we don't know where they have been on the WWW, how can the teacher have an idea about what the students know?  Schwartz [1995] speaks of the voice of the author, and suggests ways in which we might design software so as to provide very considerable freedom for readers (students) without giving them completely free range.

## HARDWARE AND SOFTWARE; PLATFORM RELIGION

A major advantage of the Internet is that teachers do not have to worry about software and hardware issues as much as in other situations.   *Netscape Navigator* is a powerful browser program available for several platforms.   There are dissemination issues.  For example, if you want your students to download a spreadsheet file, what file format should you use, and for which platform and application?

We certainly will be sending materials like spreadsheets to our students.  At the same time, we can now send them forms, have them enter data, and then retrieve their responses to our servers for crunching and reporting back.   The net result is platform independence.   If you have a controlled access system or an intranet, then you might even be able to license copies of the applications for all of your students.   I suspect that this approach will grow and change over the next several years.

Although all of the examples used in this book come from the **Macintosh\*** world, I have tried to identify the specific task that needs to be accomplished, and to describe insofar as possible the attributes that any suitable software and hardware must possess in order to accomplish the task.

Once this manuscript was in a fairly advanced stage, I tabulated all of the Macintosh software by identifying the task that was performed and the name of the software I've used to accomplish that task.   While this approach may be informative, it also is inherently unfair.   Were I working in the **Wintel\*** world, I might conceptualize and go about accomplishing a particular task in a different manner.   Readers are encouraged to remember this caveat.  Besides, the world of digital technology being what it is, many things may change between the time this book goes to press and the first copies emerge. I expect the churches of the different personal computer platforms to unify in the next decade.


## REPLACING TEACHERS WITH MACHINES

Once you have your courses totally Webified, will they still need you? I suspect the answer is yes. There are two reasons for this. Essentially no humans are good enough at self-regulation that we can learn new, difficult areas outside of our expertise without some teacher. Also, as time goes on, learners will need to know more — not less. So, it seems to me inevitable that the number of students will grow significantly as the per capita demand for learning increases. If one really believes in lifelong learning, then an attendant implication is an increasing number of students. In fact, one part of President Clinton's 1996 rhetoric has been to suggest education for all Americans through 14 years of school.


## A PERSPECTIVE

My sense is that WWW-based instruction is coming whether I think it is a good idea or not. No votes will be taken. Costs actually *are* lower. Except for a few cases — such as the United States Medical Licensure Examination — there are no quality controls in education.

> Finally, we find it anomalous that no drugs can be sold in the United States without first demonstrating, by experimental tests and clinical trials, their efficacy and safety, while publishers and schools can freely impose simplified readers and related schoolwork on children without having to produce experimental evidence of the efficacy or safety of their schoolbooks.
>
> Hayes *et al.*, 1996, p. 506

With a few word changes, perhaps the same sentiment noted by Hayes *et al.* in reference to reading materials could be applied to the likely rush to teach using the WWW. Times are nearly certain to change. Imagine renting one electronic line to your house and using that for nearly all of your communication and video entertainment. Well, not only does that appear to be what is emerging, but the costs are acceptable. USWest in Omaha already offers this service in a test market area. All other things being equal, costs will become substantially lower for those who do much international calling.

Legislators seem to be far less favorably disposed to build new schools than they were 30 years ago. This is in the face of rising construction costs but decreasing communications costs. As a result, legislators seem anxious to incur the savings likely to be created as a result of using the Internet.

I'm human, too. I'm as susceptible to face validity arguments as much as most others. A technically oriented student of mine lives in Missouri. He's a good student. For him to come to class requires a nearly 3 hour drive each way. Should he make the drive to be learning about **HTML\*** or statistics? Certainly not; you bet I'm for distance learning. But, he has a child with an extremely serious set of medical problems. Sometimes, as a result of the child's needs, he must shut down his professional life. His is a heart-wrenching situation. One could read about this on the Web. When he's your classmate, perhaps sitting near or next to him in class after he's made his drive, and the nature of these personal problems emerges as a result of some discussion — say about special needs students in schools — your view of the problem is, I believe, *much* more personal. I realize this is a face validity argument in favor of face-to-face instruction, and I apologize for my obvious lapse of objectivity.

As anxious as I am to see instruction about technical matters like becoming a Webmaster or learning statistics moved to technologically based distance formats, that's how reluctant I am to move *all* of what I and my students do to those formats. As noted earlier, my own mental view of the need for face-to-face exchanges has moved from being that these are required absolutely to that this is an open issue, one for which research is needed. My head and my heart are not in synchrony on this issue.

# CHAPTER 3

# MULTIMEDIA OVERVIEW

Designing a course involves focusing on many different aspects of instruction. Instruction is a whole and not just parts. The purpose of this chapter is to summarize the parts available for WWW-based instruction. Before turning to the parts, it might be appropriate to describe an older course that made extensive use of technology and then sketch out how that might be handled today.

## REMINISCENCE

Recent changes in multimedia have been substantial. In 1980, I spent a considerable amount of energy on "synchronized, lap-dissolve slides." *Synchronized* means coordinated by means of an audiotape — a two-track stereo system in which one track is used for monaural sound and the other for electronic signals that went to a small box containing what today we would call a computer chip. This system allowed two slide projectors to be controlled simultaneously. The two projected images were superimposed, one atop the other. Technically that was no small feat. The slides were in plastic mounts with glass covers. They contained pins to align precisely the developed slide film. Even the camera used to create the slides was impressive — a modified Nikon that accomplished pin registration thereby making multiple exposures easy to accomplish.

The purpose of going through all of this was to be able to bring successive slides to the screen, one after another, with new lines of information seeming to appear because repeated lines were so perfectly superimposed on their predecessors. Some call this technique progressive disclosure or a "text build."

Text from which the slides were produced was printed using transfer lettering systems and printing machines. The text was carefully placed on paper or colorless transparent plastic sheets which also were pin-registered. Making a set of 20 text slides such that new lines of text might seem to appear as if written on the screen might take 2 or 3 days. In addition to being quite tedious, the task also was very boring.

For each class period there was one audiotape and two slide trays. There might be 50 slides in each tray, or 100 slides. The students purchased prepared printed notes for the course so that the slide-based information could be presented at the rate of a slow speaking voice. They did not need to add much to their notes. Why use lap dissolve instead of television? Television production in those days was still more complicated and much more expensive. Indeed, one feature of the multimedia course we taught back then was to create videotapes of the slide programs that students could view repeatedly in a Resource Room. Those tapes were created by replaying the slide program on a screen and videotaping from that replay. Creating the courseware materials required a support staff of three persons employed part time during the academic year and full time during the summer.

For all the expended effort, this system was not interactive. A concurrent project I was engaged in at that time, using Control Data Corporation's PLATO to create a "lower-division chemistry course," was much more expensive though a good deal more interactive.

The presentation part of this course was very impersonal. During weekly laboratory classes, I made an effort to know each student personally — and could call about 750 out of 1000 by name anywhere on campus by the 8th week of classes. The same effort expended on classes of 200 led to quicker and better results (98% after 5 weeks), and I can claim to still know some of those students. I've spoken earlier about the serious problem of face validity — that teachers believe in strategies that have face validity whether or not those strategies work. The strategy of knowing students by name has a tremendous amount of face validity with me.

## MULTIMEDIA TODAY AND TOMORROW

Today the effort of our 1980s chemistry course could be accomplished by one person, the teacher. She could create the materials at the desktop. The total time she spent might be about the same as two decades ago — since both the production meetings and the lengthy and careful reviews seeking errors could be bypassed. If minimal television material and less than top quality are acceptable (they usually are), the overall hardware and software cost for a competent production system is closer to $5K than $10K — less than the cost of the camera and copy stand used for the earlier work!

Student access today is much easier than two decades ago. In those days a teacher couldn't count on VHS players being available in dormitories; today they can. But TV is not the dissemination medium of choice. The Internet provides a comprehensive access mechanism. Access is widely available in homes and dormitory rooms. Today distribution is easier than it was for programs that made use of videotapes. The cost of the client-side hardware has been transferred to the student (the same as with VHS players). Of course, since the teaching hardware also doubles as a device for playing electronic games, students are quite willing to ask their parents for "instructional" systems of ever increasing multimedia power. The devices students use to access the Web also play CD-ROMs. Although the ROM-based videos (today) are of lower quality than most TV, they can be made highly interactive.

Interactivity has become the really critical design issue. Interactivity implies that active learning will be encouraged. Early multimedia, even early **computer-aided instruction (CAI\*)**, wasn't very interactive. Today students can respond and receive nearly immediate feedback 168 hours per week. They can interact with media materials, make choices, type words, hear words, and so forth. Students cannot easily say things and have their words judged electronically, but that isn't far off. Students can, however, be "listened to." As described later, conferencing with the exchange of pictures and voice is likely to become very commonplace. If the throughput traffic can be sustained, it may be the most remarkable part of the telecommunications revolution in teaching. It's also likely to replace the telephone as our everyday communication device.

Today it is not difficult to have students access communications systems with one another. Establishing **listservs\*** (automatic electronic mailing systems) is becoming routine. Teachers can catalyze communications among students in ways heretofore impossible. In fact, today teachers can help to link students from different schools or countries or continents to one another.

Don't lead yourself to believe that these student communications are the same as in your current classrooms. The fundamental nature of electronic conversations is very different from what we have today as teachers. Very different. Today, the "press of the flesh" is possible. The subtle interhuman communications that sit at the core of a teacher's ability to motivate go largely unobservable using the new technologies. Teaching using this environment certainly will be different. Judging from the number of letters in the press about personal involvements developed over the Internet, it would be safe to say that different student–teacher relationships are likely (certain?) to emerge from the new student–teacher environment.

Everything in my previous teaching experience suggests to me that an impersonal Internet course with no face-to-face exchanges and no judging of individual work is unlikely to succeed — even with material as cut-and-dried as most of introductory chemistry or anatomy or differential equations. This is one of those face validity arguments; I believe it but can't support it.

## THE MEDIA

The main purpose of this chapter is to provide an overview of the kinds of media that are possible to deliver using the WWW.

Reading Texts

Discussions of multimedia often overlook text as a medium. It remains arguable that text is the second most important medium of the human condition (after speech). For scientists and engineers, it certainly is first. We communicate in writing. Most professional people communicate in writing.

As a teacher, you can expect that you'll be providing enormous amounts of text material for your students. Early on in decisions about your course, you need a good way to think about how you will handle text. New text probably will be created using a word processing program, or some other form of computer generation of text. Existing text in digital format probably can be converted into Web-useful formats as described below.

You may have a great deal of text material that is available only as print on paper. Retyping may be the best way to get this material into digital forms. Many **optical character recognition (OCR\*)** software packages (such as *Omni-Page Professional*) are available. When the text is very "clean," it can be scanned and converted into a digital format by such software. However, when the text is messy, or small amounts of text are involved, retyping is a good solution.

The appearance of text on the WWW is controlled by "marking" the text with a series of **tags\*** as seen in Figure 3.1. In fact, the files are coded in a language called HTML (hypertext markup language). Figure 3.2 shows the resulting screen.

```
<HTML>
<HEAD>
<TITLE>WWW.CCI.UNL    A Description.</TITLE>
</HEAD>

<BODY BGCOLOR=#FFFF95>
<H2 ALIGN=CENTER><A NAME="Top">
<IMG SRC="HomeHeader.GIF"   WIDTH=371 HEIGHT=95> </A></H2>
This server offers resources related to the activities of
<A     HREF=      "http://www.cci.unl.edu/CVs/David_W._Brooks
.html">David W.
Brooks</A> and his students and research collaborators at
the Center for Curriculum and Instruction, University of
Nebraska-Lincoln.<P>

Extensive construction has been and continues to be
undertaken at this site!  Please forgive errors and
inconsistencies.
<A HREF="mailto:dbrooks@unlinfo.unl.edu">
Please report problems</A>.<P>
```

Figure 3.1. Tagged HTML file (named "Default.html" located on the author's server at the University of Nebraska. See Figure 3.2. The label **http:\*** refers to the hypertext transfer protocol.

Once text is available on the WWW, two things become true. The problem of creating print copies (paper copies) is transferred from the teacher to the end user. The student relies on the browser software to create printed copy. Also, once on the Web, a quick motion of the mouse is usually all it takes to begin the process of copying the unencoded text from the teacher's machine (server) to the student's machine (client).

This server offers resources related to the activities of <u>David W. Brooks</u> and his students and research collaborators at the Center for Curriculum and Instruction, University of Nebraska-Lincoln.

Extensive construction has been and continues to be undertaken at this site! Please forgive errors and inconsistencies. <u>Please report problems</u>.

Figure 3.2.  Capture of a computer screen from the author's Web site, www.cci.unl.edu.  The tagged text in Figure 3.1 is used to create this page.

Be *very* cautious about your use of copyrighted materials.  Check with your campus bookstore or a local school printer (like **Kinkos\***).  These folks may be able to secure copyright access for Web applications when access to your server is controlled.  Before you write something, search the Web to see if something that is nearly what you would write already is available.  If it is there, you may be able to use that material instead.

## Hypertext

Using computers, and especially when using WWW-oriented software, hypertext becomes possible.  In hypertext, interacting with one bit of text, say by pointing with a cursor and then clicking a mouse button, can lead directly to different text (or other media) located elsewhere.  For example, you might have an interactive glossary set up such that when new words are introduced in one place, the user can click to obtain a definition.  Indeed, your glossary can include audio information, pictures, animations, movies, or the full gamut of "multimedia."  Traditional, unlinked text probably is the most important medium you'll use as a teacher.  With just a little experience, hypertext could take up second place in your toolbox!

This book has both a glossary and a list of software products.  Were this book on-line, then the glossary could be a work of art.  For example, the definition of hypertext could be illustrated by links to pictures, sounds, movies, Web sites, and other items.

The reason to classify hypertext as a medium is to elevate it in your thinking such that you become aware of its potential. In multimedia instruction, appropriate use of hypertext is a mark of literacy.

## Images; Image Formats

Chapter 5 is devoted to images. Images have played a key role in scientific textbooks for several centuries. Galileo used illustrations in his manuscripts of the mid-1530s. Modern textbooks, especially those aimed at large audiences, are usually multicolor affairs. Thirty years ago these texts often contained a signature (section) of color images or "plates." Today even the printed text is emphasized using color to code words in certain categories.

If you look at century-old science textbooks, you'll see illustrations that are black-line drawings. Some of these are marvelous in the way they illustrate complex concepts. Using pictures to teach is nothing new.

The WWW readily accommodates images. (Browsers based solely on text do exist, and creators of Web materials frequently are admonished to write HTML tags keeping these Web users in mind. In a world of 18-month doubling times, and in the context of the rest of the material offered in this book, you probably won't be surprised that I regard such an admonition as frivolous. There are times when, for reasons of speeding transmissions, one might set a browser so that images are not displayed, in which case creating tags that provide alternatives, brief text descriptions of what the images contain that appear in lieu of the image, may be helpful. See Figure 3.3.)

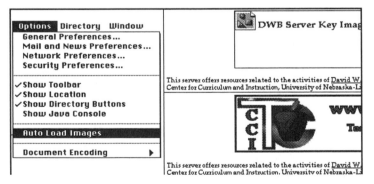

Figure 3.3. The IMG tag for this file includes the element ALT="DWB Server Key Image." At left, the browser (*Netscape Navigator*) has the "Auto Load Images" turned off. The ALT text appears (top right). When the image is loaded, it appears as at the bottom right.

Where do the image files come from? They can be scanned from photographs, captured from computer screens, produced on **Photo CDs\***, brought in as single frames from video sequences, captured by **digital cameras\***, and obtained in several other ways.

## Drawings/Paintings

**Drawing\*** and **painting\*** programs are numerous. These two classes of programs are not the same. A fundamental difference between drawing and painting is worth noting. In drawing programs, one creates equations — hidden from view — that go on to create the image. In painting programs, one creates an image **pixel\*** by pixel (i.e., screen dot by screen dot). Drawing is intrinsically easier to edit and smaller. The software permits changing the parameters of the equations, and this makes for both compactness and editability. Drawing programs include *Canvas*, *FreeHand*, and *Adobe Illustrator*. I still use *SuperPaint* more often than any of these. By most standards *SuperPaint*, a combined painting/drawing program, is old.

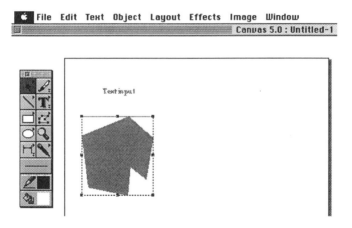

Figure 3.4. Screen capture from *Canvas 5*, a high-quality drawing program.

## Animations

In *Web-Teaching*, the term *animation* is used to indicate a sequence of drawing or graph images stitched together to form a movie. Animations are probably used as often as movies in teaching, especially when one does not count talking faces. For more discussion, see pp. 67 and 74.

## Photographs

The are numerous ways to place photographs on computer screens. These can be captured and converted into formats suitable for inclusion in **Web pages***.

## Graphs

Some of the earliest graphics programs were used to create graphs. Graphics programs today have become quite remarkable in terms of quality. Spreadsheets nearly always include graphics capability. There are, indeed, some dedicated graphing programs such as *DeltaGraph* and *KaleidaGraph*.

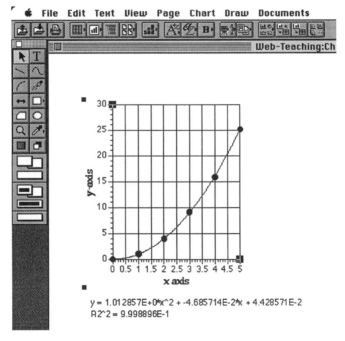

Figure **3.5.** Screen capture of *DeltaGraph Pro*, a high-quality graphing program. The data for $y$ = $x^2$ were entered with whole number values for $x$ and slight "fuzz" for $y$. The program plotted data, determined the formula for the curve, drew the curve, and estimated the goodness of fit.

## Morphs

A **morph*** is a sequence in which one image is transformed sequentially into another. In a way, morphs can be regarded as photography's answer to animation.  Morphing has become a very common multimedia technique.  It can be used by teachers to illustrate developmental phenomena.

## 3D; CAD

Computer-assisted design programs permit the creating of very exciting images, ones very useful in teaching technical disciplines.  The effects of CAD programs are obvious in some modern movie extravaganzas — as manned high-speed flight craft race over the surfaces of strange planets or vast space-bound structures.

When it comes to using advanced features such as 3-D rendering, visualization and photo realism, Macintosh CAD users seem to be evenly split between those who look to a core program to meet their needs and those who integrate functionality with third-party offerings.

With nearly all Mac CAD programs supplying some measure of 3-D functionality, and a plethora of 3-D modelers vying for the market, it is not always easy for companies to pick and choose.  Depending on a CAD program to cover 3-D can reduce training costs but also greatly increase workstation memory requirements.  On the other hand, a best-of-breed approach, which favors a variety of software, can mean higher purchase, training and software support costs, as well as problems integrating different file formats.

Streeter, 1996b , p. 37

As with so many other kinds of software, companies marketing 3D and/or CAD programs are anxiously flooding the marketplace with products aimed at the WWW.  Some of these focus on the creation of images for use in Web documents.  Others seek to greatly empower users.

## Special Programs

Some special programs have been created for specific disciplines.  In chemistry, there are several programs for creating images of molecular structures.  These may be represented in any of several ways, such as with letters (alphameric characters) representing atoms and lines representing the chemical bonds between atoms, or with three-dimensional spheres touching overlapping spheres representing three-dimensional molecular structures.  Examples of this sort are illustrated in Chapter 7.  Expect to see an increase in the variety and power of special programs made available for the WWW.  The ultimate objective will be to sell software to professional users.

## Movies

Movies are sufficiently important that they are treated separately in Chapter 6. On the one hand, movies can make representations of the world available that are difficult or impossible using other media, especially text. Movies represent a great challenge, however, since the necessary **bandwidth\*** (network capacity) is very large.

## Sound

Sound will be treated in Chapter 7. There are at least six different ways in which sound can be used in multimedia programs:

- Music
- Audio tracks of instructor voice, just as if recorded from a lecture
- Text to speech tracks in which text files are "spoken" in a computer voice
- Earcons, sounds that indicate a particular operation or convey some constant information
- Informational sound, the nature of which indicates some special meaning about the data
- Live radio-like sound

A teacher can record lectures, and have these audio tracks available over the WWW. For visually impaired students, this may be particularly helpful. In most teaching situations, sound is not very useful. One can record the sounds made by a scientific instrument, or the calls of a bird, and put these to extremely good use, for example.

## Virtual Reality

Visual aspects of virtual reality are coming more and more to the fore. For example, software has been developed that will permit you to tour a museum. You can interact with visual information that will take you into the museum. Once "inside," you can turn around to see the choices or options of where to go, and choose a hall or exhibit area. You can seemingly walk here and there and, when inside a particular gallery, scan its contents. You can zoom in on (walk up to) individual exhibits in the museum. For example, the following text appears at a Web site advertising a software product aimed at production of virtual reality materials for WWW distribution:

> 3-D Website Builder is the easiest WYSIWYG way to create the coolest "Virtual World" site on the Web without programming. Unlike flat HTML pages, VRML Worlds created with 3-D Website Builder allow visitors to walk through your site and virtually see where they're going and where they've been. This life-like spatial quality

makes it easier and more exciting for visitors to navigate without getting lost among hundreds of flat pages. In addition, a 3-D World is several times more efficient than a flat Web page since each 3-D room has at least six 2-D surfaces to place content.

With 3-D Website Builder you can design your own virtual store, create a virtual family photo hall of fame, give the press access to your virtual press room, allow your distant family to take a virtual walk-through of your new house, encourage visitors to tour your virtual trade show, invite exploration of your virtual 3-D campus and more.

Virtus Corporation, URL J

Although virtual reality materials can be developed at this time, the serious limitation is that file sizes are large; there is a bandwidth problem when adopting them for WWW-based instruction.

## Touch

It is possible to use touch as a medium of instruction. Special gloves, for example, can connect the user to a world of tactile surreality. As of this writing, touch is not yet ready for prime time (i.e., the WWW).

## Smell

Don't bet that smell won't be used during your lifetime. I suspect that it still is a long way off, however. Nevertheless, my guess is that as these words are being written there are basement laboratories with modules of digitally controlled chemical reservoirs and researchers figuring ways to control the release of mixtures of scents.

If not this approach, would you believe surgically implanted electrodes that ... ?

## Taste

Expect taste soon after smell. Watch for an electrode palate!

# CHAPTER 4

---

# WEB-READY MATERIALS

A teacher needs an understanding of how things are accomplished on the WWW so as to be able to design good materials — and providing this understanding is the intent of this chapter.

While designing Web materials is exciting and can be fun, making them "happen" on the WWW requires a rather sophisticated but much less stimulating set of skills. Today ordinary mortals create some rather extraordinary media with the help of powerful computer applications tools. You need to go to other resources to learn about the details of creating individual files. For example, to learn about HTML code you can either search the Web or purchase any one of scores of books on the subject.

You can use your browser to open the coded source of any HTML file your browser looks at as a text file, and to save/edit/modify that file on the browser's machine. (Surfers on the Web *can* copy your pages, but they *can't* modify or edit them on your server.) Authors, therefore, can't hide their code from you, so that when you see something brilliant on the WWW, you nearly always can figure out how the author accomplished that effect. Sometimes you're even able to help yourself to enough code to create a template for yourself — allowing you to create files that duplicate the desired effect at will.

## THE MIME SYSTEM

**MIME\*** (Multipurpose Internet Mail Extensions) is an extension to the traditional Internet mail protocol that permits communication of multimedia electronic mail [Grahan, 1996, pp. 619-627]. These are defined in document RFC (Request for Comment) 1521. Servers send document "content-type headers." The MIME system permits the server to "know" what to send. When the client receives the file, it "reads" the header to know what kind of content it must deal with. These operations are accomplished as the result of using the file name extensions. Computer platforms (UNIX, Windows, Macintosh) handle this problem in slightly differently ways.

MIME is a standardized scheme that permits browser software to determine what to do with a file. The file is assigned an extension written as a few letters and a period or dot. Files ending in .html or .htm, for example, are interpreted as being tagged text. Files ending in .GIF are **GIF\*** image files, while those ending in .jpg or .jpeg are **JPEG\*** images. A file ending in .hqx has been encoded (in a format called BinHex 4.0) so that it can be transferred from machine to machine. Once moved, the encoded file must be decoded before use. Applications and document files are transmitted via the WWW using this strategy. (Moving files over the WWW is an alternative to the more widely known **ftp\*** strategy.)

The HTML-tagged file will call other files. The browser uses the extension to decide what to do with the files. The browser may make use of **helper applications\*** and/or **plug-ins\***, computer programs designed to interface the special document with the browser software (Figure 4.1). These are assigned or set up in the browser.

What is a Plug-in? (From: Netscape: Architecture)

Plug-ins are dynamic code modules, native to a specific platform on which the Netscape client runs. Plug-ins are intended to be complementary to platform-native inter-application architectures such as OLE 2 and platform-independent programming languages such as Java. The primary goals of the plug-in API are to:

Provide seamless new data-type support for Netscape users
Provide the maximum degree of flexibility for plug-in developers
Be functionally equivalent across all platforms

The current version of the plug-in API supports four broad areas of functionality. Plug-ins can:

Draw into, and receive events from, a native window element that is a part of the Netscape window hierarchy
Obtain data from the network via URLs
Generate data for consumption by other plug-ins or Netscape
Override and implement protocol handlers

URL  K

There may be special helpers required for some of the resources you want to distribute. For example, Cambridge Scientific has a plug-in used for browser-based manipulation of *ChemDraw* and *Chem3D* files. These applications and plug-ins can be downloaded by your students from the WWW, but when you are requesting them to use something specific, you might make an alternative source available to them — consistent with copyright rules, etc.

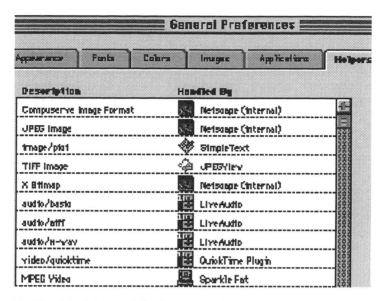

Figure 4.1. Identifying helpers and plug-ins. Access the General Preferences menuitem from the Options menu of *Netscape* to display this screen.

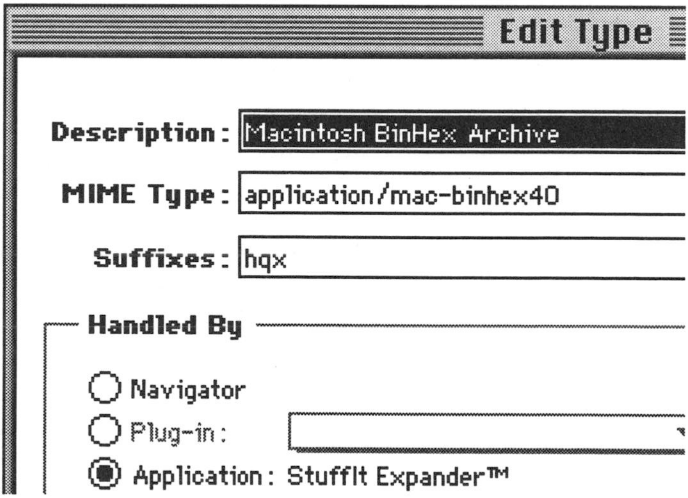

**Edit Type**

**Description:** Macintosh BinHex Archive

**MIME Type:** application/mac-binhex40

**Suffixes:** hqx

**Handled By**

○ Navigator

○ Plug-in:

● Application: Stufflt Expander™

Figure 4.2. Choosing Edit Type for one of the helpers (in this case, Macintosh BinHex Archive, a scheme for converting files to enable moving them over the WWW) allows suffixes to be entered/edited, and an application or plug-in chosen to assist the browser by handling the files involved. In other words, any file with a .hqx MIME suffix is assumed to be "binhexed" and is opened with *Stufflt Expander*.

## HTML; MARKING TEXT

Controlling the appearance of text in a WWW browser is by no means a sure thing.  What the end user sees is a function of the HTML file, the client software being used, and the options chosen by the user.  Modern word processing and desktop publishing programs, as well as others, usually are aimed at creating on the screen what will appear in print (**WYSIWYG\*** — what you see is what you get).  If teachers give word processing files to their students, then both should see the same things on their computer screens.

That's not usually how WWW publishing works.  When the primary task is to make very transportable files in a machine-independent system, making the learner's screen look like the teacher's screen presents a substantial problem.  In 1996, the WWW uses a text markup language.

The computer files created by modern software, when examined on a byte-by-byte basis (Figure 4.3), actually contain numerous seemingly bizarre charac-

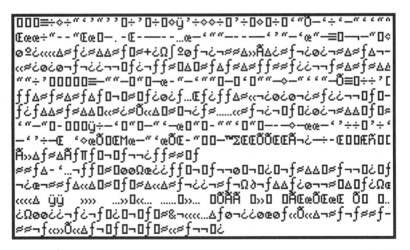

Figure 4.3.  Screen capture of a portion of an *MS Word* file used to create this book.  The file was opened with a text editing program (*BBEdit*).  The character stream means something to *Word*; it means nothing to nearly all human eyes.

ter strings that are used by the software program to convert the file information into WYSIWYG material.

For some user to see on his or her screen what the creator of that document saw or sees (that is, for them to share the same WYSIWYG), each must have the same software program to make sense of these coding character strings.  The proliferation of programs creates problems.  What if your word processing program is not the same as that of your student?  In this situation, we might be able to acquire some software that converts, say, a *Word* document into a *Word-*

*Perfect* document. Powerful programs often include converters of files from other formats into their own format. To get different printers to create similar printed documents, the printers need somehow to make sense of these characters — and perhaps to convert them into different characters understood by the printers. One such printing protocol is *PostScript*, and many word processing programs create and send *PostScript* files to printers.

The system used in the WWW is different. Here the text files are marked or *tagged* such that *all* software programs intended for Web use will read them and interpret them similarly. While this is more a dream than a reality in a world of precise standards, the culture of Earth in the mid-1990s accepts this approach. Over the WWW, things can look similar from one screen to another — but they may not necessarily appear identically (Figure 4.4).

This creates a different problem for the author of Web materials — how to create text files that are marked suitably. The currently used language is HTML (hypertext markup language).

There are many ways to go about obtaining HTML-tagged text for your materials. One is to learn the various tags, and type them using your favorite word processor. Then, save the file as an **ASCII\*** text file rather than in the normal format for that software. The simplest of word processors, like *SimpleText*, are up to the task. I've become very fond of a text editing program that includes tools for tagging the text. In its current incarnation, *BBEdit 4.0* creates color-coded text in a manner that I find quite convenient. Special tools automate nearly all of the tagging. I must know what the tags do, but I don't need to remember the details of those tags. I employ this text editor instead of a word processor to create the HTML files I use. One of the tools allows me to "click" the current text file into my browser. Without this feature, one can save the edited file, and then open that file with browser software. That's a bit more involved, but it accomplishes the same outcome.

You may purchase word processing software that includes tools for converting files to HTML-tagged text files. *WordPerfect* has such a feature, as does *Nisus Writer*. These work by having you create your WYSIWYG word processing file, and then having software convert that file into an HTML-tagged text file.

Another way is to use software that simplifies the text tagging process — a sort of Web word processor. In this case, the WYSIWYG is based upon some hidden tagging of a text file and interpretation of the tags much as a browser might interpret them. *Visual Page, PageMill, PageSpinner*, and Netscape *Navigator Gold* are such programs.

An emerging strategy is to make extensive use of small Java applications (**applets\***) within Web pages. *Coda* is intended as an application that creates WYSIWYG Web pages *entirely* as Java-based material. The HTML files it creates consist of a few lines that call the Java applet. *WebBurst* is one of several applications that facilitate the creation of Java applets for inclusion within Web pages.

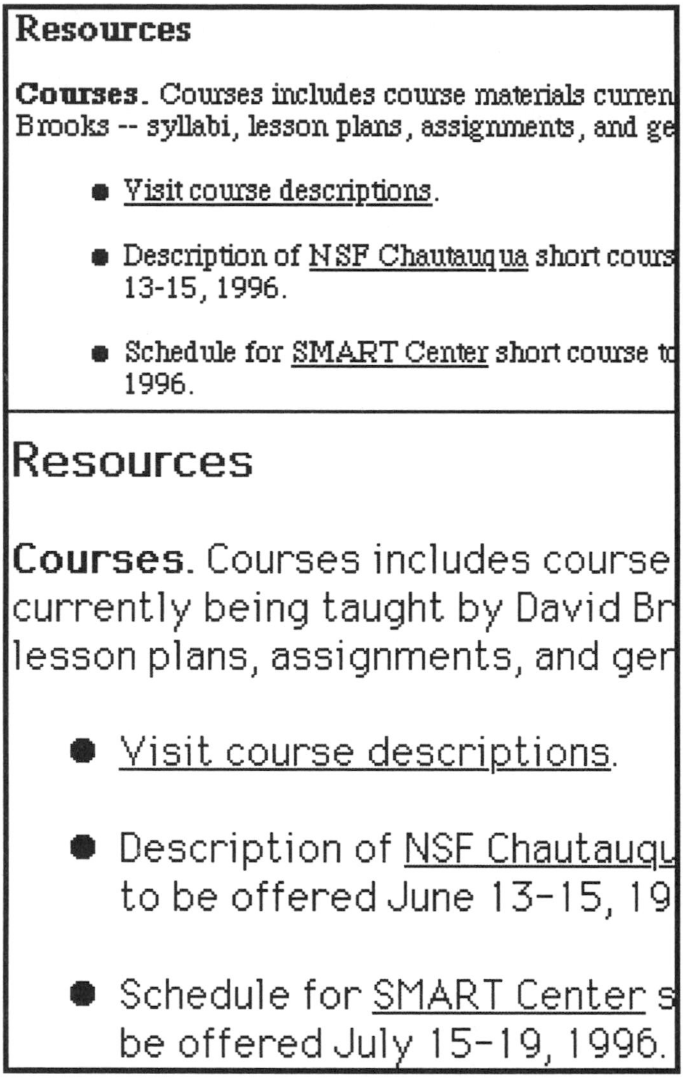

**Resources**

**Courses**. Courses includes course materials curren
Brooks -- syllabi, lesson plans, assignments, and ge

- Visit course descriptions.

- Description of NSF Chautauqua short cours
  13-15, 1996.

- Schedule for SMART Center short course t
  1996.

# Resources

**Courses**. Courses includes course
currently being taught by David Br
lesson plans, assignments, and ger

- Visit course descriptions.

- Description of NSF Chautauqu
  to be offered June 13-15, 19

- Schedule for SMART Center s
  be offered July 15-19, 1996.

Figure 4.4. Two views of an HTML-tagged file opened with the *Netscape Navigator* browser. The views differ in the font type and size setting chosen by the user. On the WWW, you must work very hard to control exactly what the user sees. Most often, users don't see exactly the same screens as the author because of differing font and/or background color defaults.

Still another strategy is to use whatever software you might normally use to create a document, and then print that to a "**metaprinter\***" that interprets the documents' codes as if to print them but creates tagged text instead. *Myrmidon* is software that attempts this sort of tagged file creation.

Many companies are adding applications to handle the encoding of a document into HTML. Microsoft offers a product, *Internet Assistant for Microsoft Word*, that handles conversion of documents created in *Word 6* (Windows 95, Windows NT, Windows 3x, and Macintosh) into HTML-tagged files intended to produce Web pages that look about the same as the WYSIWYG produced by the *Word* document.

There was an evolution in my use of software for HTML files. I used a **shareware\*** program that added code visibly; I saw the tags. When I began tagging text, programs like *Visual Page* (*PageMill, PageSpinner, Navigator Gold*) that hid the tags did not exist. After a while, coding became so much a part of my skill set that a program like *BBEdit*, with all of its related HTML tools, became very easy for me to use. Most student coders with WYSIWYG tagging software don't try to compete with me when coding. One reaches a point where the slow step involves thinking about how you want the screen to look, and any good software tagging system serves to implement your design. Ultimately, when you have lots of materials at a major site, you will need to know enough about code to go in and repair or adjust code. In this event, tools like *BBEdit* are invaluable. The impact of applications that create Java applets as a part of the page creation process remains to be determined. Those applications have an exciting look and feel to them, and the pages they create are flashy. When teaching, I demonstrate the use of *SimpleText* to create an HTML file. I don't recommend this approach. Some dedicated software — either a text editor with appropriate tools, or a WYSIWYG program — is essential.

There is a great deal of busywork involved in creating appropriately tagged text. It is complicated by the fact that graphical browsers are not quite interchangeable. Some browsers create and implement HTML standards without the concurrence of the official authorizing organization. (Netscape has become such a potent force that it can do this — and get away with it.)

Although *Navigator Gold* edits tagged files, I don't use that program for tagging. I have adopted the practice of saving edited files directly to the server; *Gold* expects the file and the application to be on the same volume, and I don't want more software running on the server than is absolutely necessary (so that server performance remains high). All I would need to do to make this work would be to edit on my desktop machine and, once the file is finished, move it to my server.

## Going Partially Digital

There are other ways to "go digital" with your course, some of which have a chance to prevail. Paper is still a good medium for teachers; it is still the easiest text format to take to bed or to a park bench. Many things students are expected to learn require either a great deal of concentrated study, or a great deal of reading. Paper is a good medium in both of these situations because of portability. Don't forget paper. Don't forget books.

Several products are available to create files such that having the file and an appropriate software reader program enables both cross-platform electronic WYSIWYG viewing and printing across platforms as well. *Adobe Acrobat* is one such software family. Had the reader program for *Acrobat* initially been freeware, then penetration of this software might have been greater. If you want to use this, then you create your materials with whatever software you want — *Word*, *WordPerfect*, *Quark*, and the like. Then, when the file is as you want it, you "print" it to the *Acrobat* software that creates the generic files (a **.pdf\*** file). These are the files you distribute to your students. The students use their reader software to bring the files up on their computers. If they want hard copy, they print those files. Several companies have gone to distributing manuals for their software electronically, especially when they distribute disks. My Kodak DC50 camera came with two sets of disks, one for Mac and one for Windows. Both sets contained software for processing images, and a .pdf file manual.

With very low-cost metaprinters making HTML tagging into a "printing" operation, I suspect that other formats and alternatives won't survive in their present form. You'll likely use your favorite software to create the file you want, and then "print it" to create an appropriately tagged HTML file. If that file doesn't do what you want, you'll edit it a bit with a text editor. It is my view that doing so is not wise but you may, if you choose, keep essentially all of the HTML encoding hidden from yourself in a black box.

## LINKS

A very key idea in the HTML scheme of things is the way in which *links* are created. Hypertext is enabled readily thereby. The nature of the link is explicit and is usually encoded in a cumbersome text string. The nitty gritty of hypertext is hidden in most programs that afford hypertext capability. Links are there for all to see in the HTML text file. In the browser screen seen by the user, however, links are divulged only by clear but still subtle changes in the text format — usually colored, underlined text.

The links in a WWW browser can bring about quite simple changes — with a link in one part of a document connecting to another part of the same document. The user clicks on a linked text string, and the screen images change displaying a different portion of the same document.

The power of the Web is that the links point to documents that can be downloaded from servers literally continents away. The power of the browser software is that suffixes attached to files can be used to invoke "helpers" and "plug-ins" that enable a full range of multimedia applications. That programmers can make use of this strategy enhances greatly the potential of the Web and the utility of browser software. It also is true that if the user doesn't have a good conceptual model of what is going on in the WWW, it can be very confusing.

## The Anchor Tag

Perhaps the most important of the "tags" in the HTML is the anchor tag, <A> ...</A>. Two important attributes may be included within an anchor tag.

### HREFs

The HREF attribute within the anchor tag is used to indicate the URL for a hypertext link.

```
<HTML>
<HEAD>
<TITLE>Test.html</TITLE>
</HEAD>
<BODY>
<A HREF="#Brooks">Go Brooks</A>
<A HREF="http://www.cci.unl.edu">Go Brooks'
site.</A>
<A
HREF="http://www.cci.unl.edu/CVs/CVs.html#Brooks">
Go Brooks at Brooks' site. </A>
</BODY>
</HTML>
```

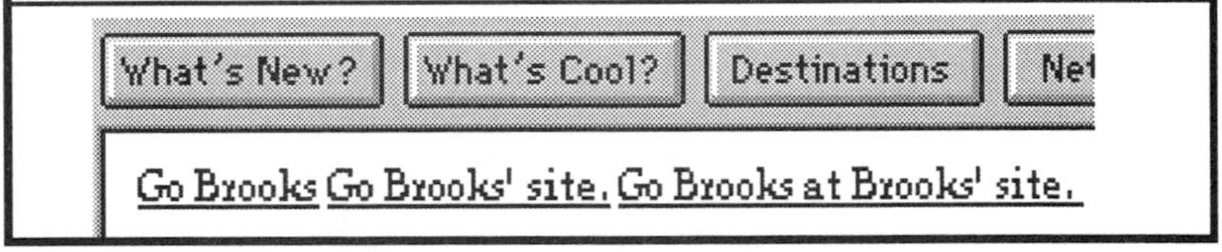

| What's New? | What's Cool? | Destinations | Net |

Go Brooks Go Brooks' site. Go Brooks at Brooks' site.

Figure 4.5. Top: HTML file with three links. Bottom: appearance of this file as displayed in browser. The first link goes to a named place within the current file. The second goes to a different file, likely on a different server. The third goes to a named portion of a different file on the same server where the second file is located.

### Names

The name attribute within an anchor tag is used to name parts of text for access via hyperlinks. The name tag shown below would name the word *Smith* somewhere in a file with the label "Smith" so that it could serve as a hypertext link.

<A NAME="Brooks">Brooks</A>

## IMAGES

WWW browsers handle an image by using a tag that references the file for the image:

<IMG SRC="GIFs/AceticAcid.GIF">

Images are discussed in Chapter 5.

## MOVIES

Adding a movie to your work involves creating an anchor that tells the browser where to find the file and, using the proper MIME extension, which helper to use once the file is transferred. An anchor that calls a movie is:

A short <A HREF="LegoMan2.mov">scene in LegoLand. (600K)</A>

The appearance in the browser is:

> Cat Binki chasing a laser dot. (3.3M)
>
> A short scene in LegoLand. (600K)
>
> What the kids did with/to the QuickCam... (689K)

A captured image from the movie is:

Movies are discussed in Chapter 6.

## TRANSFERRING FILES

Transferring a file, as noted earlier, is accomplished by using an anchor with the file location and the appropriate MIME extension.

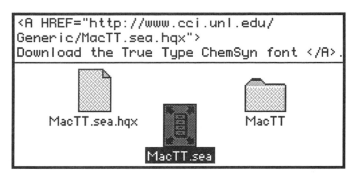

Figure 4.6. Top: Anchor used to download a BinHexed file. Bottom: Icons of three files. The file MacTT.sea.hqx is stored on the server; it is this file that is copied and moved. Once the file copy has been completely transferred, a helper application (in this case *StuffIt Expander*) "unbinhexes" the file producing MacTT.sea. Then this application is decompressed (with *StuffIt Expander*) giving the folder MacTT.

One of the biggest issues about transferring files deals with cross-platform problems. If you're using a Mac server, how can you serve well those of your students who have Windows machines? There also are differences within a given platform based on differences in browsers. *Navigator*, *Explorer*, and *Mosaic* can give quite different screen images.

# CHAPTER 5

# IMAGES

This chapter discusses many issues specific to images and the WWW.

## LAST STEP; SAVING IN A SUITABLE FORMAT

The last step in creating an image file is saving it in an appropriate format and with a MIME extension. Some applications accomplish this task directly.

Two file formats are commonly used for the Web. The GIF file, developed by CompuServe, permits up to 256 colors. There are several ways in which GIF files can be created so as to make them especially friendly for the WWW. The GIF format once was thought to be in the public domain, but a series of legal actions emerged that clouded its potential use [Morgan *et al.*, 1996, pp. 145–146]. GIF formats, nevertheless, are widely accessible on the WWW. The other format commonly in use is JPEG. JPEG permits **compression\***. JPEG files may contain up to millions of colors. A JPEG file needs to be decompressed by the browser. *QuickTime* by Apple, available for both Macintosh and Windows systems, deals with JPEG handsomely. The WWW is evolving so quickly that, fairly soon, virtually every common image format will be usable. Also, considerable effort is being expended to create a new format (PNG) that deals with files in similar ways to the GIF format [Eaton, 1996; URL B].

Software programs are available that take files from just about any platform and/or format and convert them into any other platform/ format. Getting existing digital images into a WWW-suitable format is not that great a challenge. In the worst case, one can open a file on a suitable machine, copy it to some transient memory (like the **clipboard\***), and then paste the image into a program that will save it in an appropriate format.

I copy files to the Macintosh clipboard and paste them into a file program that saves in the desired formats. I've been very satisfied with the shareware program *GIF Converter*. Another program that comes highly recommended is

*Debabelizer.* I've used this program too, with considerable success. There are other commercial and shareware programs as well.

## GIF Wizard

Net resources are available to optimize GIF files — cut them down in size. One such tool is GIF Wizard available at Raspberry Hill Publishing [URL AJ]. One enters a URL for the GIF file to be optimized. To get the URL for the file to be optimized using *Navigator*, open the file that calls the GIF on your server with *Navigator*, move the cursor into the GIF, and press the mouse. When a menu pops up, choose "Copy this Image Location." The URL for the GIF is copied to your clipboard; paste it into the appropriate place at the GIF Wizard site, and click the "Magic" button. The GIF Wizard goes to your site and copies your GIF file. Then a series of optimizations are performed on your exported image. You can see how they look on your screen. If one of them looks good and saves space, you can copy it back to your site. To do this, move the cursor into the new GIF at the GIF Wizard site, press the mouse, and choose the menu option "Save this Image as ... ." You can name the new file and direct it to the desired location.

Figure 5.1. This image was captured from a browser's screen created by opening the file below.

It is important, when you save a file, to save it with the appropriate extension (.GIF or .jpg). When using *BBEdit* to create my HTML-tagged files, all I need to do is use the dialog box to "find" the desired file. *BBEdit* does the rest, including finding the height and width of the desired file.

```
<HTML>
<HEAD>
<TITLE>Showing an Image Tag</TITLE>
<H3 ALIGN=LEFT>Image Tags</H3>
The purpose of this file is to show
<BR>readers how an image tag is encoded.<P>
<IMG SRC="TC.GIF" ALT="Teachers College
Graphic" WIDTH="124" HEIGHT="93"><P>
That's all there is to it!<BR><HR>
</HEAD>
<BODY>
</BODY>
</HTML>
```

Figure 5.2. This file was used to make the Web page, the main portion of which was captured to produce Figure 5.1.

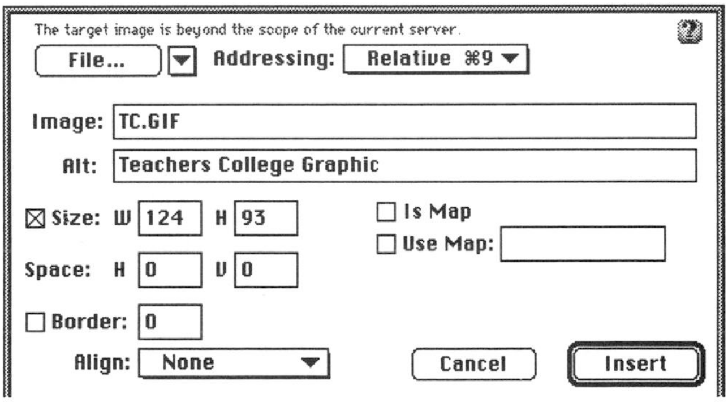

Figure 5.3. This HTML helper, available in *BBEdit 4.0*, was used to enter the image tag. Locate the cursor where the image should appear relative to surrounding text and click. Bring up the dialog box using the *BBEdit* HTML extensions. Note that the image size is loaded automatically. Also, note that a text alternative is included in the tag.

The image width and height are included to permit the browser to move the text into position while saving appropriate space for the images. Then it can go back later and fill in the pictures. All in all, this speeds user access.

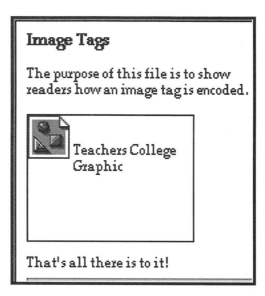

Figure 5.4. If for some reason the client browser is not autoloading images, or the image is not available, the "ALT" in the image tag provides a text description for the user. Browsers using the Web from home over a slow **modem\*** may routinely turn off image autoloading.

## GETTING THE PICTURES

How do you obtain the pictures themselves? There are many routes depending on whether you are starting from scratch or converting an existing source.

### Scanners

Use a scanner when you have a photograph or a printed image source (magazine). Keeping in mind copyright restrictions, some magazines regularly publish images useful for teaching. *Science*, for example, regularly publishes quality images useful for teaching biochemistry and neural pathways, two of my interests. *Scientific American* has some terrific artwork. (Releases are needed for both publications.)

As of this writing you can purchase a good bottom-of-the-line color scanner for under $400. This will typically have a resolution of 300 × 600 dpi. Scanners today can give much higher resolution, and offer other features as well (Figure 5.5). Today you can find scanners capable of scanning out essentially all of the information contained in a photograph.

Many software packages are available to help to scan images and process the results. *Photoshop* is such a program, a widely respected tool that is rather easy to learn to use but also very powerful. It is useful for beginners, and for professional artists as well.

A scanner also can be used to move printed text into computer-editable files. You may have older sets of notes in printed form that can be scanned and then converted using an OCR (optical character recognition) program.

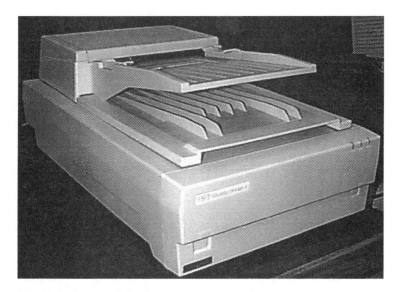

Figure 5.5. Flatbed scanner (SilverScanner III).

## Photo CDs

An extremely good way to capture still images, one for which enormous technologies have been developed over a century, is film. Today 35-mm cameras and modern films afford tremendous potential for capturing appropriate images. Individuals and universities often own considerable camera gear, and there are many gifted amateur photographers among our faculty, student, and staff ranks.

The Kodak Photo CD offers a simple and, in my view, inexpensive way to capitalize on the extant hardware, film, and knowledge. One can take existing slides or film negatives, and send them to a laboratory for transfer to a Photo CD. My own experience involves sending exposed film (print film) to a laboratory and receiving developed film and Photo CDs in return.

The standard Photo CD can hold about 100 images. Software on the Photo CD permits you to examine each photo. Five different image magnifications are available. The greatest resolution demands enormous amounts of memory, and provides what is tantamount to magnification of the image (Figure

5.6). You can almost see the grain of the photographic emulsion at the highest Photo CD resolution.

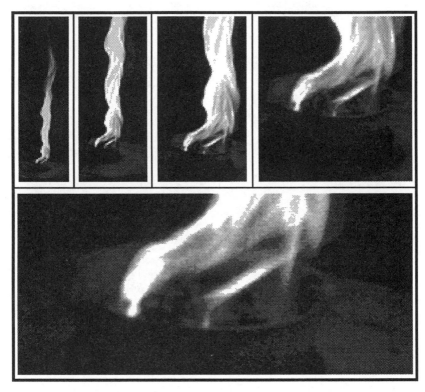

**Figure 5.6.** Five resolutions available from a Kodak Photo CD. Top, left to right, in pixels for the image: 192×128, 384×256, 768×512, 1536×1024; bottom, 3072×2048. Image of a luminous flame from a burning hydrocarbon placed in a porcelain dish with a piece of paper towel. The original Photo CD is in attractive 24-bit color.

At the time of this writing, the entire process had a cost of approximately $1 per image. When one does a great deal of work digitizing images, one appreciates this low price. Kodak also sells software that permits manipulation of the image quality. My co-workers have had a great deal of luck with Kodak software. Even the way in which Kodak returns the Photo CD offers convenience. Typically there is a numbered thumbnail color image in the jewel box for the Photo CD that permits quick review of the images for the purpose of locating any particular desired image (Figure 5.7). If you need images right away, the Photo CD is not your solution. This is a 4-hour to several-day solution. It takes time to develop film and to create the Photo CD. If you need images in an instant, you'll need to use either a digital camera or some sort of video capture system.

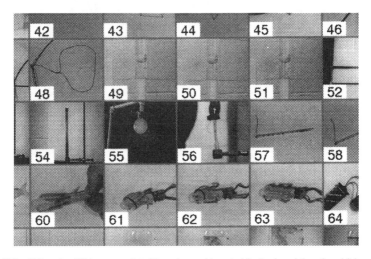

Figure 5.7. "Thumbnail" images printed in color and inserted in the jewel box in which a Kodak Photo CD is delivered. These facilitate use of the CD.

## Digital Still Cameras

Several companies make digital cameras; their cost is a function of the resolution and other features. Apple sells a low-resolution camera, the QuickTake. Several companies, particularly Panasonic, sell high-resolution cameras. We are very impressed with the cameras offered by Kodak. The Kodak DC50 camera (Figure 5.8) is both versatile and easy to use. The accompanying software permits facile modification of the resulting images.

I use a 4-Mbyte flash memory card with my Kodak DC50 camera which allows for storage of about 40 images of "better" quality among the choices good, better, and best. Usually as I work, I transfer the images from the camera to a computer hard drive. (Transferring the images is slow — it takes a few minutes to move ten pictures.)

A perfectly good question would be, why bother? Digital cameras save a step. They give rapid turnaround. So, from start to finish, going from real-world phenomenon to digitized image, you can have what you need in minutes rather than days. The cameras are portable. Most of them offer higher-quality images than can be obtained with corresponding TV cameras — since they have greater inherent resolution. Many images in *Web-Teaching* were created using a Kodak DC50; for example, Figure 5.9. Digital still cameras have been reviewed in several magazines (URL L).

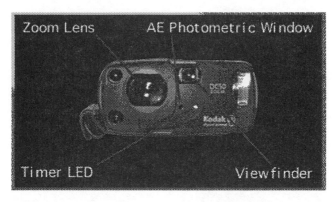

Figure 5.8. A screen capture of a picture showing the Kodak DC50 taken from the Kodak Web site. Start at http://www.kodak.com.

Video Frame Capture

Using an appropriate board or other converting device, single frame video images (analog output) can be converted into digital still images. For nearly 5 years I used a Canon Xapshot camera that captured still frame images as video. These images, 50 of them, were recorded onto a small floppy disk held in the camera. When using the AC power supply, one could pop out one disk and pop in another (the battery wouldn't last for more than 50 or so images). The analog images from the Xapshot were converted into digital formats using an external device called *ComputerEyes*. This system served well. The Xapshot recorded color video, but I nearly always needed B&W images. The Xapshot resolution is ultimately lower than that of a Kodak DC50 camera. Also, the Kodak software makes image manipulation easier than does the *ComputerEyes* software. Live video could be fed into *ComputerEyes* with the same result as the Xapshot, except for the "talent" needed to remain very still for 3 to 4 seconds while the image was obtained.

AV computers have since come to the fore equipped with boards capable of capturing images. Two factors limit the quality of computer desktop video. One is the quality of the videocamera, and the other the speed with which a board can capture, compress, and store the video. My current system, a Power Macintosh 8500/180, has both in and out ports for video, S-video, and stereo sound. I can attach a video camera to the computer and then, using software such as *Apple Video Player*, capture single frames. Many other third-party solutions are available. An interesting, popular, and very inexpensive solution is the Connectix QuickCam (p. 99). The Color QuickCam "can take still pictures in millions of colors at 640 × 480 pixel resolution. The fast, manually adjustable focus lens provides sharp images from less than 1-inch to infinity and is optimized for indoor lighting."

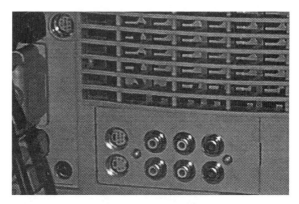

Figure 5.9. Video connectors at rear of Power Macintosh 8500. S-video, video, and stereo sound — both in and out.

## SIMPLE ANIMATIONS

Once you have images, you can do some things with them. One easy effect to accomplish is to paste a series of images together to make an animation movie. Using *GIF Animator* software, it is an easy matter to stitch GIF images together. These can play as a loop on a browser screen with no special added applications. The effect I've used is to make a series of images of molecules using *Chem3D* and rotations of about 15 degrees each. When stitched together into a new GIF file, the result appears as a movie that can play continuously. When used with rather complex structures such as proteins, the effect can be dramatic.

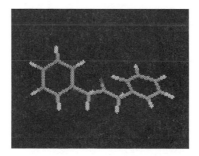

Figure 5.10. Animation from the Web site used by Nick Turro for his freshman-level organic chemistry course. At the time this screen image was captured, Professor Turro had been using his Web site for only 3 months! [URL W].

## CAD

Computer-assisted design programs permit the creating of very exciting images, ones very useful in teaching technical disciplines (Figure 5.11). The effects of CAD programs are obvious in some modern movie extravaganzas — as manned high-speed flight craft race over the surfaces of strange planets or vast space-bound structures.

Figure 5.11. Architectural renderings offered by ArCAD UK, a British company that advertises its design services using the Web. Captured from: http://members.aol.com/arcaduk/frame.htm.

## CREATING VIRTUAL REALITY PROGRAMS

It's difficult to know where to place virtual reality in this book — with images or with movies. Figure 5.13 shows two pictures captured from a series taken in the student laboratory where I work. Elizabeth Petrakis placed a digital still camera on a special tripod and captured images sequentially as the camera was rotated through 15-degree increments. These images are then stitched together to create a file that is interpreted by *QuickTime VR*. By moving the mouse while pressed, a virtually continuous display is presented as if one were standing in the center of the laboratory and continuously turning around. The rate is determined by the extent of the mouse gesture. This is something you must see to believe. It can crawl, or it can spin at a dizzying rate. In order to run this with *Navigator*, you need the *QuickTime VR Components* plug-in. Access to this tool is available at Petrakis's site.

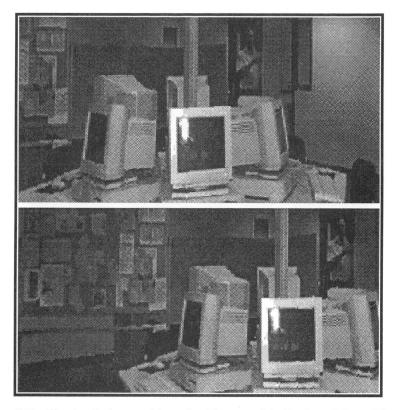

Figure 5.13. Virtual reality images of the student laboratory of the Teachers College, University of Nebraska. This display was created by Dr. Elizabeth Petrakis, and is available at a UNL page. [http://www.unl.edu/tcweb/Faculty/petrakis/EPTechlab.mov].    Created    using    *QuickTime    VR Authoring Tools Suite 1.0.*

## MORPHING

Morphing is another animation technique made easy by computer.    In morphing, two images are blended in such a way as to create the effect that one image is being transformed into the other (Figure 5.12).    So, replacing the face of a man with the face of a woman is simple.    One uses the morphing software to create the intermediate images, and then stitches these together into a movie or uses them appropriately as a series of stills.

**Figure 5.12**. A simple morph created quickly using *Elastic Reality*. This morph could be entitled "Generations."

# CHAPTER 6

# MOVIES; DESKTOP TELEVISION EDITING

The impact that **digital technologies*** have had on television is nothing short of remarkable. The surrealism that greets viewers is spectacular. This has been made possible by computers. Nothing is more spectacular, however, than the decrease in costs associated with television production. Today desktop television is an achievable reality. In principle, one person can do in minutes work that used to take many hours or even days to accomplish.

While this is very true, desktop television is not something to enter into casually. There are two reasons for this. Costs of top-quality systems are still quite high; desktop television may be something you don't want to "own." Also, all of those folks who were involved with older television productions were not just human robots performing routine tasks. Most were able to bring a sense of production quality to the task. If you are a teacher of some discipline, don't assume that you can bring high production quality to the desktop.

In spite of these caveats about cost and quality, many teachers have decided to undertake their own television production. What teachers do bring to the task is a sense of the troubles students have when they encounter material. This knack for identifying the teaching stumbling blocks is key in many situations.

## INPUT QUALITY

The process of digitizing video materials is one that inherently degrades quality at each step. It can't be overemphasized, therefore, that the best final products emerge when the starting "footage" is of high quality. Aspects of quality are many. For example, the images needed must be on the tape! The tape must have captured what was needed. Unless your video tools are very powerful, the video must have captured the information well — it must nearly fill the video screen, and be devoid of distracting visual information. So, step one involves some kind of minimum quality in videography.

Technical issues must be addressed, too. When you shoot home video with a consumer-quality VHS recorder, the playback quality may be adequate for home use. For digital work, however, you'll want to start with recorded tape of a much higher resolution. This means shooting at least Hi-8 or SVHS formats. Equipment for both of these formats is a good deal more expensive than ordinary consumer equipment. What you get for this effort is more lines of horizontal resolution. There is more information on the tape when you start those transfer and copying processes that inevitably introduce noise and thereby degrade the information.

Digital video cameras promise to capture video information digitally rather than by using an analog process. Costs and performance of these new systems remain to be determined in the marketplace. An examination of various home pages such as from Panasonic (www.panasonic.com) shows products with descriptions such as the Panasonic PV-DV1000 digital camcorder. Rumor has it that starting prices will be low enough to stimulate massive consumer demand soon after the units are introduced.

## HARDWARE

If you shoot your own video, you'll need a camera and recorder (or camcorder). This will be at the top of your hardware list. If you have a source of videotape, you'll still need a way to play it.

If the available video is not in digital format, the first task you face is to digitize the video. (You can use appropriate hardware and software to create what essentially is a master digital tape from raw analog input. However, when creating any WWW multimedia, digitization is inevitable.) The hardware involves a video capture board and a computer. The computer and the board must work well together. Because of the enormous amount of information involved, the computer must be very fast, and storage capacity must be extremely large. Ordinary video runs at 30 frames per second. To capture all of the information available at that rate is a substantial technical challenge. Indeed, virtually no system tries to do this; nearly all systems perform some sort of data compression at the time the video is digitized.

Compression procedures can be **lossless\*** or **lossy\***. Lossless means that the information can be precisely reconstructed from the compressed data. Lossy means that some information is lost in the compression step. Nearly all video compression is lossy.

At the end of video compression, you're likely to have a hard drive with one or several *very* large files. The remaining task is to edit and modify those files so that a useful teaching product results.

## SOFTWARE

Once the files of digitized video are on your hard drive, you're ready to begin the process. You will need to use some nonlinear videoediting software. **Drive space\*** and **RAM\*** can limit what you are able to do. These are operations where a 1-gigabyte drive and 48 megabytes of RAM specify a smallish system.

Software packages allow you to open and view video. You can easily cut off the ends of a sequence. You also can cut something out of the middle.

Whether you're an expert or a beginner, you can easily create high-quality digital movies and videotapes with Adobe Premiere(R) software. This powerful editing program lets you combine video, animation, still images, and graphics to bring your ideas to life.

Adobe Premiere Web Site [URL X]

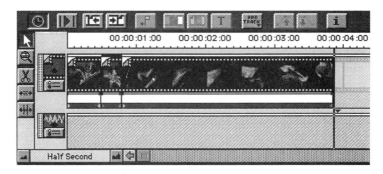

Figure 6.1. Screen capture from *Videoshop*, a nonlinear TV editing program with functionality similar to *Adobe Premiere*. *Videoshop* allows you to edit clips, combine clips with video effects, and add soundtracks. Although powerful tools, these would be regarded as being toward the bottom end of what is available today.

Many visual effects are available to go from one tape segment to another as you splice them together. For example, you can have a cross-fade — where the first images fade to black as the second images come up from black. Also, you usually can control several soundtracks at the same time.

As it happens, adding information to the video — titles, arrows, animated arrows, and the like — is quite a bit more complicated and beyond the scope of the simplest editing programs. Again, by way of advice, most teachers tend to overdo "effects." Remember, your video is embedded in a multimedia platform that can deliver information in many ways. Perhaps you ought to keep your tapes simple. Think about first focusing students on what is important, and then adding complexity. Real-world complexity cannot be avoided in most situations. Recognizing an ecological relationship in the field is a great deal different than recognizing it in a clean video. In general, however, you'll get better learning if you focus on the key points at first, and then provide situations of increasing complexity from which students must disembed the phenomenon of interest.

## COMPRESSION STANDARDS

There are two videocompression standards commonly in use. The JPEG standard, achievable using software only, creates files that are substantially larger than those created using the **MPEG\*** standard. Until recently, MPEG was much more difficult to create. As with most such situations, the technology is steadily improving, and MPEG is likely to become much more commonplace. This is very important for the WWW, as file size always translates into a bandwidth issue. You may create a wonderful movie for student use that moves over your campus network at respectable speeds. If your student at home logs in using a 14.4K modem, however, movies may not be appreciated. As with most other similar technology problems, this one, too, is expected to go away; bandwidth will grow. As of this writing, however, bandwidth is a very real consideration.

## ANIMATIONS

As noted earlier, the term *animation* is used here to indicate a sequence of graphic images stitched together to form a movie. Animations are probably used as often as movies in teaching, especially when one does not count talking faces. Animated graphs, for example, provide clear indications of phenomena. One of the most dramatic representations I've seen is a map of the counties of Nebraska, each with a three-dimensional bar whose height represents the population [Lavin, 1995]. When these maps are strung together on a decade-by-decade basis (see Figure 6.2), the impact of the U.S. Interstate Highway System becomes apparent. Completion of the interstate highway (I-80) through the state was followed by what could best be described as a phenomenon of magnetism — with the population moving ever closer to that roadway. This is a particularly effective use of animation; the movie of charts slowly plays out on the screen giving a strong visible perception of change.

## TALKING FACES

Capturing a talking face on video usually is a poor choice for teaching. When real time is not a part of the consideration, then the quality of talking face images can detract from the student's experience. Although you can use talking faces, it probably is a great deal better to use still images of the speaker and su-

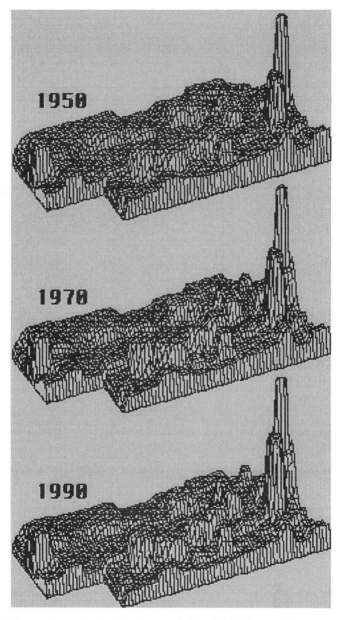

Figure 6.2. Frames from animation showing population of Nebraska counties over four decades. The data were provided courtesy of Steve Lavin, Copyright © 1995, Steve Lavin., UNL Geography Department, and modified by DWB to accommodate print publication. See text. With permission.

perimpose voice. You can accomplish this by making movies using the video-editing software in which the video image is a still, or by putting an image in an HTML file and having a link to corresponding sound be located nearby. In any case, there will be a step for downloading either the movie or the sound file.

## DIGITAL VIDEO

As noted earlier, digital video is on its way. In this approach, video is captured directly in digital format; there is no analog-to-digital conversion process required. Digital videorecording will make an enormous difference in the kinds of technology in use. That's where the boundary ends, however. From an instructional point of view, this new technology should be transparent to the teacher designer. True, we might get higher-quality video, but, for the most part, current video is more than adequate for our tasks and expectations. For teacher-video producers, digital videorecording may make life a great deal simpler!

## MORPHS; VIRTUAL REALITY

These topics were covered in Chapter 5. They could easily have been included in this chapter because both of these effects most often end up, in WWW multimedia materials, as movies.

# CHAPTER 7

# OTHER MEDIA

## SOUND; RECORDING SOUND

There are several ways in which teachers can choose to include sound in instructional programs:

- Music
- Audio tracks of instructor voice, just as if recorded from a lecture
- Text to speech tracks in which text files are "spoken" in a computer voice
- Earcons, sounds that indicate a particular operation or convey some constant information
- Informational sound, the nature of which indicates some special meaning about data
- Live radio may be broadcast over the Web. For example, one of the presidential debates was available in this format.

Remember, it can take nearly as long to download sound as to download movies! In some situations, however, sound may be well worth the use of bandwidth.

## Music

There are two things I urge you to keep in mind about music. First, it takes a long time to download music over a slow line. If speed of transmission is an issue in your teaching situation, think twice about including music unless that is what you are teaching. Second, be concerned about authorship and copyrights for background music. The best procedure is to pay a competent music student a small amount of money to create original music for you such that you own the copyright, and then use that music. Aside from these two caveats, enjoy.

## Spoken Text

Again, use of your spoken voice will be very expensive in terms of bytes downloaded. If you think spoken voice is important, then consider making a movie (like a *QuickTime* movie) that consists of still pictures (such as your picture) with voice superimposed. Don't make a movie of yourself talking; the video quality is likely to be *very* disappointing when viewed over low-end hardware. In your "voice movie," you can include several images. Since you may want to use this during situations when you feel the content is very emotional, make the interpicture transitions slow "cross-fades" rather than abrupt "cuts."

## Electronic Text to Speech

The quality of text to speech on computers has been improving steadily. To my ear, it's up to the level of fair — still less than good. If you feel that spoken words are essential, consider this option. If possible, try this on your target audience. Put your first impressions aside when deciding whether spoken text is enhancing the learning environment. You can expect many Java applets to be created to handle this task.

## Earcons

An earcon is a sound used to indicate some action. My computer nearly always beeps when I mess up. That's the Macintosh way. Sounds can be used to indicate that a process is complete, that a new page has opened, that form information has been mailed, and so forth Earcons often are built into **hypermedia\*** programs, and they are likely to find appropriate roles in Web-teaching.

## Sounds That Convey Information

My colleague John Flowers has experimented with the use of sound to convey information [Flowers and Haver, 1995]. So, when quantitative graphical information appears on the screen, there is an accompanying sound that informs the viewer of a summary of the information represented in that graph. This is a potentially powerful multimedia application.

## Radio

Live radio may be broadcast over the WWW. The 1996 vice-presidential and one of the presidential debates took place during my class about using the WWW; several of us listened at our computers as we worked at other tasks.

## RECORDING SOUND

When you include sound in your materials, one thing that is necessary is to be able to record and edit sounds conveniently. This requires some sound editing software, such as *SoundEdit 16* (Figure 7.1).

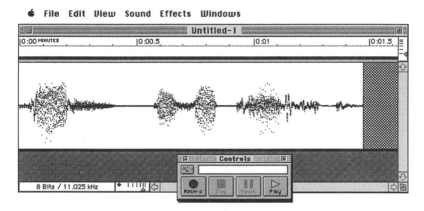

Figure 7.1. Screen capture from *SoundEdit 16* software recording the statement "this is a test." *Sound Edit* is a very powerful audio capture and editing program.

*SoundEdit* has a feature that permits saving sounds as *QuickTime* movies (Figure 7.2). This is an attractive feature since *QuickTime* is a cross-platform software strategy for the WWW. For example, the file may be opened and played using *Movie Player* or some other *QuickTime* player.

Figure 7.2. Screen capture of the file SoundTest1 saved in *QuickTime* format using *SoundEdit 16* and then opened with *Movie Player*.

## INCLUDING SOUND IN PAGES

The more time I spent working on writing material about including sound, the more I felt that providing extensive information on this issue would be unwise. Sound is a very complex area — nothing like delivering images where two or three formats cover nearly all current situations and are available for nearly all systems. An excellent reference to get you started is Morgan *et al.* [1996, Chapters 33 and 34].

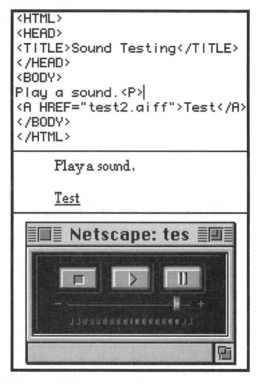

Figure 7.3. Top, HTML code to include sound. Center, screen capture of browser window calling sound. Bottom, controller window created when sound link clicked.

I decided to recommend the strategy summarized in Figure 7.3. First, get your sound file into an ".aiff" format. You can use this in Mac, PC, and UNIX worlds. Next, place this file in the server. In the case of Figure 7.3, the sound file is placed at the same level as the HTML file. Open the file using browser software to bring up the page. Then click on the link to have the sound play. It seems to me that using sound over the WWW still is a lot less convenient than, say, using sound in *HyperCard*.

## SPECIAL PROGRAMS; CHEMISTRY-SPECIFIC EXAMPLES

Some special programs have been created for specific disciplines. In chemistry, there are several programs for creating images of molecular structures.

These may be represented in any of several ways, such as with letters (alphameric characters) representing atoms and lines chemical bonds between atoms, or with portions of three-dimensional spheres (space filling models) representing the three-dimensional molecular structures.

These chemistry programs actually are specialized drawing programs. They are extremely effective in capturing chemical thinking, however, and in automating tasks key to chemists. Today the WWW provides chemistry teachers means for transmitting images of molecular structures. Some providers offer tools such that the teacher can serve a small file that permits the student opportunities to manipulate a structure. Creating the structure requires the full package; changing its display features or twisting and turning it requires only a freeware plug-in. Expect to see an increase in the variety and power of special programs made available for the WWW.

One of the best sites I've come across that can be used to illustrate structure tools in a setting that affords active learning is at the Colby College Chemistry Department [URL M]. They are using the plug-in *Chime* from MDL Information Systems, Inc. [URL N]. Liz Dorland of Maricopa College has devoted a WWW page to collecting addresses of *Chime* sites [URL AC]. Visiting her site brings up numerous excellent links showing strategies for using *Chime* software.

A typical screen found in the organic stereochemistry area [URL O] is shown in Figure 7.4. Students are shown pairs of closely related structures drawn with a structure drawing program (such as *ChemDraw* or *Chemintosh*) and asked to identify the relationship between the structures. Using the available features, the student can bring up three-dimensional representations of both structures in several forms and manipulate them. The student can, at any time, see what the relationship is by clicking an answer button. The Colby pages do not perform any assessment, but could easily be made to do so.

When one considers that, as of this writing, most Web site designers have been at the task for less than 2 years, the amount of progress to date is nothing short of fantastic. Near the end of the time I was a graduate student, one could get a good-paying summer job creating three-dimensional models for use in research. There were many colored plastic spheres, many metal rods, and much hole drilling. Although the computer tools needed for these displays have been around for over a decade, sharing this kind of material with students has been very expensive. Now the same electronic tools that bring students other Web materials bring them access to chemistry tools with this great power. My view is that this necessitates changes, fundamental changes, in the core curriculum of chemistry. It is my sense that essentially all technical disciplines are similarly affected by these kinds of digital technologies.

The software strategy behind modeling, although extremely elegant and powerful, is available as freeware and shareware. An application named *RasMol* is available from freeware/shareware sites [URL P]. Files with appropriate information about atoms and their positions are interpreted by this program to cre-

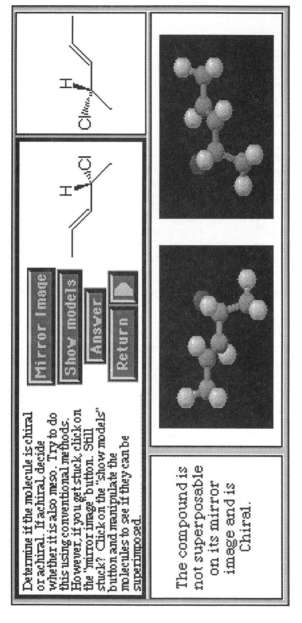

Figure 7.4. Modified screen capture of an exercise page from the stereochemistry help section of the organic chemistry portion of the Colby College chemistry site. http://www.colby. edu/chemistry/OChem/STEREOCHEM/index.html. Students have a task and are able to use all of the features described below.

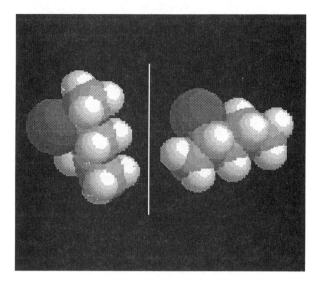

Figure 7.5. By pressing the mouse and quickly moving it, the model can be "rotated" on the screen. Once it has started moving, it can be placed in nearly any orientation desired.

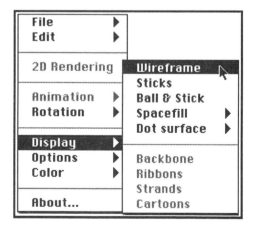

Figure 7.6. Pressing for several moments pops up a menu from which the users may select the form of the model displayed. Many choices are available.

ate windows showing molecular structures in various formats that are readily changed and rotated. These are remarkable tools!

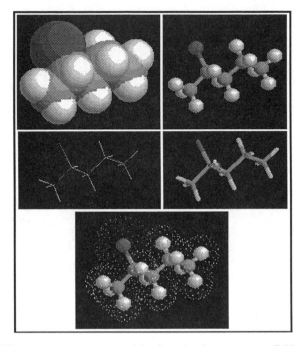

Figure 7.7.  Different ways to represent models of a molecular structure available to students.

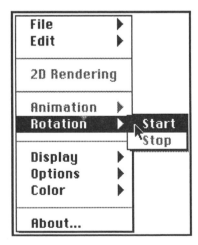

Figure 7.8.  Many options are available in this remarkable software.  By starting "Rotation," each model can be made to rotate continuously.

## ACCESS TO APPLICATION SOFTWARE

Accessing computer application software may turn out to be where the real action is on the WWW. *Mathematica* is a wonderful program that performs mathematical operations. In its most recent incarnations, this program has become very sophisticated. When using *Mathematica* (Figure 7.9), teachers create "notebooks." Text and figures surround the functions of *Mathematica* in these notebooks such that users can vary parameters in the functions to display the

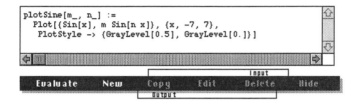

Here is an instance of the function with the values *m* = 3 and *n* = 5. You can edit these values to experiment with different plots. Each time click Evaluate.

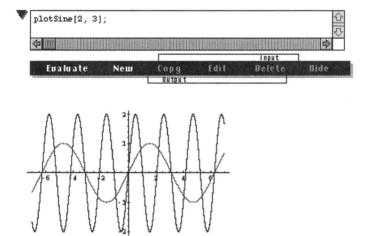

Figure 7.9. *Mathematica* screen capture from URL AB. This site permits on-line calculation and plotting. First, click evaluate on the upper menu to define the function. Then, type in suitable values for the constants *m* and *n*, and evaluate using the new values. The graph is redrawn. Little time is spent in computation; most of the time is spent in traffic back and forth over the WWW. (This notebook was created by David Fowler.)

outcomes. Today it is possible to upload notebooks to a site that not only makes them Web-displayable, but also permits interactivity. In other words, a WWW user can access a file using a Web browser, modify parameters within that file, process, and observe the outcome. This is a remarkably powerful feature, one likely to be expanded and emulated by many other programs.

# CHAPTER 8

---

# ENCOURAGING WEB-BASED DISCUSSION

This chapter deals with the value of student discussion, and the Web-based wherewithal to support and encourage discussion. It would be hard to fault an approach to devising new systems of learning, such as when planning to use the WWW as a communications vehicle, that begins with a review of what seems to work. In the opening chapters, the work of Pressley and McCormick [1995] was cited several times as a source of suggestions about teaching. The *Handbook of Research on Improving Student Achievement* offers both generic suggestions and content-specific suggestions for consideration.

Chapter 2 — Generic Practices
  Parent Involvement
  Graded Homework
  Aligned Time on Task
  Direct Teaching
  Advance Organizers
  Teaching of Learning Strategies
  Tutoring
  Mastery Learning
  Cooperative Learning
  Adaptive Education

Walberg, 1995, pp. 7–19

Chapter 7 — Mathematics
  Focus on Meaning
  Student Use of Calculators
  Small-Group Learning
  Opportunity to Learn
  Number Sense

Concrete Materials
Openness to Student Solution Methods and
    Student Interaction

Grouws, 1995, pp. 97–109

Chapter 9 — Science
    Learning Cycle Approach
    Cooperative Learning
    Analogies
    Wait Time
    Concept Mapping
    Computer Simulations
    Microcomputer-Based Laboratories
    Systematic Approaches in Problem Solving
    Conceptual Understanding in Problem Solving
    Science-Technology-Society
    Real-Life Situations
    Discrepant Events

Gabel, 1995, pp. 123–143

As one reads these lists, one suspects that similar work in different fields goes forward concurrently under different names and labels. The strengths of the research bases for these various strategies vary. Some are quite good; well-implemented cooperative learning, for example, can lead to substantial learning improvements.

I've tried to divide the instructional design tasks with respect to student interaction into two major areas: one deals with "discussion" (this chapter) and the other focuses on interacting with content effectively and exchanging information between student and server (Chapter 9). When teachers of subjects that involve extensive classroom discussions speak about using the WWW for teaching, they most often imagine that the instruction will consist of some kind of content dissemination but no discussion. Quite to the contrary, *nearly all of the early uses of the Internet for teaching have involved electronic discussions* (text exchanges): teacher–student discussion and/or student–student discussion.

Not being immune to the impact of face validity on my own teaching choices, especially as incubated in the environs of a curriculum and instruction department, I've held the view that instruction involving certain types of discourse could not be successful on the Internet. I place a high value on face-to-face contact. Both emotionally and intuitively, I believe that most learning situations demand such contact. My experience with distance learning for adults, as well as that of my colleagues, has provided evidence to the contrary. It was during the preparation of material for *Web-Teaching* and especially when reading *Learning Networks* [Harasim *et al.*, 1995] that I became disequilibrated. That is, I began contemplating what I knew about this issue rather than what I felt (and still feel) about it. This chapter deals with issues related to exchanging electronically the ideas and information generated by students.   My view has evolved.   I'm now open to the idea that face-to-face contact may not be a required element in discussion.   Remember, discussion is not the only thing that is enabled by face-to-face meetings.   Much other information is communicated between teacher and students, and among students.   Discussion, not lecturing, is the most important activity that teachers can engage in during face-to-face meetings.

Technically speaking, when considering digital strategies, discussion is easier to accomplish than is interactive content dissemination.   For discussion, what matters most to the teacher is not what is done with the Web server, but how one designs learning activities.   Two examples of recent discussions held in classes on my campus are shown.   The first came in response to a mathematics question posed in an upper-division/graduate course, and the second as a response in a lower-division history course:

> Question: A subset $A$ of the metric space $X$ is called *path connected* if, given any two points $x, y \in X$, a continuous function $\gamma : [0,1] \to X$ can always be found such that (i) $\gamma(t) \in A$ for all $0 \leq t \leq 1$, (ii) $\gamma(0) = x$, and (iii) $\gamma(1) = y$. The map $\gamma$ is called a *path* from $x$ to $y$.
>
> 1. Prove that the disk $\{z \in \mathbb{C} \mid |z| \leq 1\}$ is path connected. (A picture would help your proof, and I'll be impressed if you can post it!)
>
> 2. Prove that a path connected set is connected.

Student Response:
"To prove that the unit disk is path-connected just draw a segment of radius joining the origin with both points. Then the path consisting of these two segments connects these two points and of course lies inside the unit circle. A path-connected set is connected, since otherwise preimages of open sets disconnecting $A$ also would be disconnected open subsets of $0,1$ and since the interval $0,1$ is connected there must be a point belonging to the interval $0,1$ which is also in neither of preimages. That contradicts to the fact that the path lies entirely inside the set."

Teacher Question: "In class, I'd like us to take a close look at John Eliot's constructed dialogue between a converted Indian and his unconverted relatives (2:1).   How much does this document reflect Eliot's perceptions, and how much does it reflect Indians' perceptions?"

One of several student responses: "... I also believe that Eliot's account is mostly of his own creation.   He portrays the unconverted Indians as almost comical in their ignorance.   In Eliot's account, they are concerned with nothing but eating, drinking, and being merry, when in fact, most Indians had a very meaningful spiritual life.   The converted Indian in this account is also less than realistic.   He visits relatives living in his former village, yet he seems completely withdrawn and detached from their way of life."

The responses I've selected are intentionally brief and concise. Many times during the discussions, students challenge one another's statements. There is noticeable development of their ideas over two or three discussions.

For nearly two decades, another colleague, David Hibler, has advocated publishing student writing. Our campus has student writing contests that are judged "blind." Over the last 5 years, Hibler's students have won at least 10 of the 15 available prizes, even though there probably are 70 writing instructors on campus. Beginning in the fall 1995 semester, all of his students published all of their writing on the Web. They sign releases to do this at the beginning of the course, and then again at the end to permit maintaining their contributions on the Web. So far, none have declined. They publish anonymously. Hibler has a system whereby students can send and receive e-mail anonymously. The Web publishing and anonymous electronic commenting represent new wrinkles in his approach which he believes, on the basis of anecdotal evidence, enhance student learning. Hibler teaches very elementary HTML tagging during the first week, and students submit tagged files for assessment. His students usually write about 20,000 to 30,000 words each during the semester. Hibler's students follow publication with interactive anonymous commentary about one another's anonymous work. Since the framing questions Hibler begins with elicit autobiographical writing (the first three of ten warmup themes, for example, are "The Me I Am," "The Me I Was," and "The Me I Envision"), the responses become very personal and very deep in no time. In fact, after 2 weeks in his class this semester (fall 1996) the last passage of one student's writing was to the effect of "I can't believe I've just written this."

Hibler has quite a different view of hypertext than I do. My view is that hypertext is linked text — such that one concept or idea can lead to another in nonlinear fashion. He sees hypertext in terms of cycles where writings on a topic, once published, lead to more and more writing on the same topic. Thus, the view of one generates views from many.

There are at least two issues to be concerned with about discussion. The first involves the design of the instruction. The early efforts seem to me to be resulting in very positive learning outcomes (face validity). As of this writing, the colleagues whose work I've described had only begun thinking about posing questions and encouraging discussion over the Web. My guess is that the results after 5 years will be still more powerful. The second issue concerns how a teacher would set up some computer implementation of these exchanges, and hence this chapter section. (Chapter 4 of *Learning Networks* is a very good reference for readers of *Web-Teaching* interested in considering a variety of interactive teaching strategies centering on discussion, questions, and answers [Harasim *et al.*, 1995].)

## COOPERATIVE LEARNING

Many innovations in education are discarded as fads. Cooperative learning is a strategy with quite strong research support [Ellis and Fouts, 1993]. It is likely to stick. (The Keller Plan gave good results, but didn't stick [Pressley and McCormick, 1995]; one never can be sure.)

In cooperative learning, learners are held responsible to one degree or another for their fellow learners' learning. *Web-Teaching* is not intended to be a primer on cooperative learning. All of those issues aside, it is an easy matter to use the Internet as a means of helping to implement cooperative learning. Just by using e-mail and group mailing addresses where three or four students easily can mail to one another, teachers can create very successful groups. In testing out some of my ideas for this book I chatted with many researchers named herein, and was easily able to follow through with e-mail. That's an example of cooperative learning! Students can use e-mail in the same way. As noted earlier, teleconferencing will be useful for support of cooperative learning.

Once I taught a course for high school chemistry teachers using the Internet. A qualitative study of the course interpreted cooperative learning as one of the most powerful features [Liu, 1996]. To tell the truth, all I did to make this happen was to create a listserv from the outset, and to make the first assignment be to have everyone introduce themselves on the listserv. The participants all were chemistry teachers, and most K–12 teachers know about cooperative learning. Realizing the worth, they made it happen for themselves.

A note of caution. Effective cooperative learning for inexperienced learners — like most college freshmen and most high school sophomores — demands considerable teacher planning. Also, while much research will emerge, there is no assurance that a strategy that works face to face will work over the WWW. If you are new to cooperative learning, find someone who uses cooperative learning to teach the same content and level that you teach, and discuss your plans. In other words, seek an experienced mentor for developing cooperative learning strategies, preferably one who has been successful in your discipline and with students similar to your own. Plan your Web-based approaches after those conversations. A very good place to find collaborators is on the Web itself. There are ongoing teacher discussion groups for nearly all disciplines.

> Attention to instructional design is one of the most critical factors in successful learning networks, whether course activity is delivered totally or partially on-line or in adjunct mode. All education, on a network or in a face-to-face environment, involves intervention by an expert (the instructor) to organize the content, sequence the instructional activities, structure task and group interaction, and evaluate the process.
>
> Harasim *et al.*, 1995, p. 125

I suspect that videoconferencing between students will become a major means for accomplishing cooperative learning. In fact, I suspect students discover this for themselves in many courses where there is essentially no tele-communications component whatsoever; it will replace the phone!

## SUPPORTING WWW DISCUSSION

If you intend to have discussion at a distance or over time, you'll need some ideas about managing the related technology.

### E-mail — Simple and Effective

Teachers probably should be using e-mail in all courses whether or not they have a presence on the WWW. E-mail can become the principal tool for maintaining interactions between students and teachers in many settings. Sawrey [1996] has used e-mail for years. She tells her students that she will log on daily at least once between 10 P.M. and midnight to respond to questions. When she stays at meetings on the East Coast, this entails some late night hours for her. Her students usually send mail to her between 5 P.M. and 4 A.M., a timing schedule she attributes to their e-mailing at the time of studying the material. Software programs she was instrumental in developing include "buttons" that permit students to e-mail quickly and easily to instructors.

The most compelling point she makes is a comparison between e-mail traffic and live traffic at her office during office hours. Few students visit her office; many contact her through e-mail. Most of us who teach at research universities find little traffic during office hours unless we introduce some gimmick — like insisting that students pick up graded exams during office hours, or some such thing. With no data to support this, my sense is that e-mail should be coupled with those gimmicks that bring students in for one or two visits per term.

I use e-mail to maintain frequent contact with student teachers. A minimum of two weekly communications is expected, and the creation of a daily journal with entries for 2 or 3 days transmitted in each e-mail. In other courses, I used to accept and encourage e-mailed assignments, but these days I insist on them — in much the same autocratic fashion that my freshman composition instructors demanded that all of my papers be typewritten.

### Listservs

Listservs are automatic mailing lists. Mailing something to a listserv causes that message to be mailed to all e-mail addresses subscribing to that list-serv. My experience in this area centers on an Internet-delivered course taught during the spring of 1995 concerning the use of small-scale laboratory activities when teaching high school chemistry. I used two channels of communication: e-mail directly between me and individual students, and a listserv. A listserv was easy to set up. Readers of this book probably subscribe to several listservs.

In fact, you've probably unsubscribed from one or more listservs so as to reduce the volume of material coming your way. The following student comment from my chemistry course listserv was in response to an experiment description and data posted by another student. The flavor of this comment is just about exactly the same as I observe when I teach that material in workshops with face-to-face discussion and hands-on laboratory contact.

> MaryHelen's information on the Charles Law experiment looks very good. Could you please tell us whether this data was collected by you (MaryHelen) or your students? If it was your students, could you give us an idea of the time it took for them to get set-up properly? How about comments from them as to how easily they were able to get the pipet set-up with the colored water drop, etc.

Institutions usually run software for listservs on large computers. Software for desktop computers is available. In a sense, *ListStar* does for lists what *WebStar* does for the WWW in the Macintosh world.

Every teacher probably should set up some kind of listserv or discussion group for nearly every course — unless the enrollment is one! I use the equivalent of a small listserv — a special mailing address — for graduate students in my research group. (A listserv is a better way to handle this because it is easier for the students to share communications with the group. Without a listserv, I must relay messages from individual students to the class. New students may not have the needed information to set up groups for their mailing software, however. It works out better for all concerned if I manage organizing a course listserv.)

Most of the listservs I'm "on" are for chemistry teachers or educators. As one might expect, there are Web sites that provide lists and other information about listservs (Figure 8.1).

It is my sense that students at many levels should be encouraged to participate in listservs.

## UserNet; News Groups

When a listserv develops a great deal of traffic, you might want to consider changing to a user group or news group. A listserv offers automatic e-mailing so that all of the traffic comes to each member. Each must choose what to read and what to discard from his or her computer. In a news group, messages are posted on some server that is accessed by a news reading program. The user ultimately chooses which of the posted messages to open and read. News groups are inherently cleaner than listservs; the user takes what is desired, rather than discards what is not desired. Listservs are appropriate for most teaching situations; news groups usually are unnecessary.

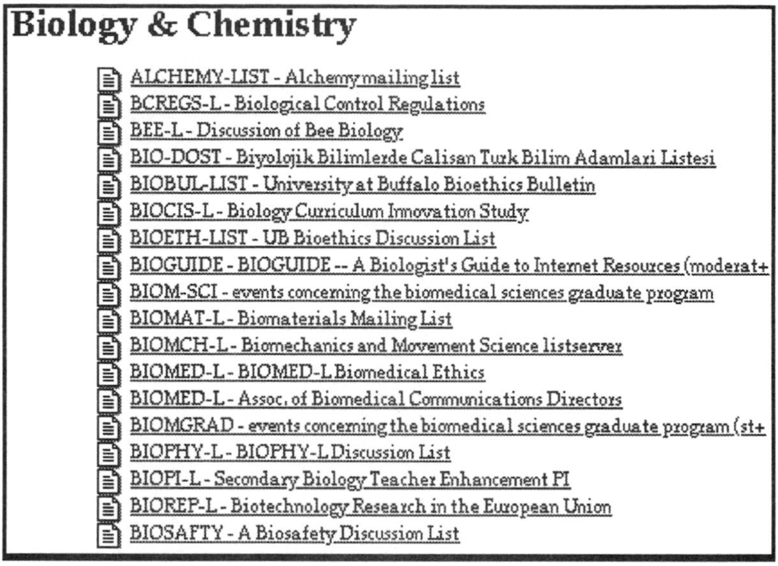

**Biology & Chemistry**

- ALCHEMY-LIST - Alchemy mailing list
- BCREGS-L - Biological Control Regulations
- BEE-L - Discussion of Bee Biology
- BIO-DOST - Biyolojik Bilimlerde Calisan Turk Bilim Adamlari Listesi
- BIOBUL-LIST - University at Buffalo Bioethics Bulletin
- BIOCIS-L - Biology Curriculum Innovation Study
- BIOETH-LIST - UB Bioethics Discussion List
- BIOGUIDE - BIOGUIDE -- A Biologist's Guide to Internet Resources (moderat+
- BIOM-SCI - events concerning the biomedical sciences graduate program
- BIOMAT-L - Biomaterials Mailing List
- BIOMCH-L - Biomechanics and Movement Science listserver
- BIOMED-L - BIOMED-L Biomedical Ethics
- BIOMED-L - Assoc. of Biomedical Communications Directors
- BIOMGRAD - events concerning the biomedical sciences graduate program (st+
- BIOPHY-L - BIOPHY-L Discussion List
- BIOPI-L - Secondary Biology Teacher Enhancement PI
- BIOREP-L - Biotechnology Research in the European Union
- BIOSAFTY - A Biosafety Discussion List

Figure 8.1. This screen listing biology and chemistry listservs is accessed via the home page: http://www.tile.net /tile/listserv/index.html.

# CHEMCOM

**Chemistry in the Community Discussion List**

Country: **USA**
Site: **State University of New York at Buffalo**
Computerized administrator:
**listserv@listserv.acsu.buffalo.edu**
Human administrator:
**chemcom-request@listserv.acsu.buffalo.edu**

You can join this group by sending the message " **sub**
*CHEMCOM yourname*" to listserv@listserv.acsu.buffalo.edu

Figure 8.2. Screen capture of information about the ChemCom listserv provided at the site noted in Figure 8.1.

```
Date: Wed, 23 Oct 1996 09:00:35 MDT
Reply-To: chemed-l@mailer.uwf.edu
Sender: owner-chemed-l@mailer.uwf.edu
Precedence: bulk
From: xxxxxxxxxxxxxxx
To: chemed-l@atlantis.cc.uwf.edu
Subject: Re: Scientific Writing Sample Needed

I use the 1935 issue of the Journal of the
American Chemical Society as a good source for
experimental analytical data on inorganic and
organic compounds for general chemistry
problems.  It is a nearly ideal source for the
scientific writing samples you want as well.

Sincerely,
Xxxx Xxxxxx
```

Figure 8.3. Text of a message from the ChemEd-L listserv. This message is a response from a frequent contributor to an earlier question regarding scientific writing. When it comes to content, this contributor is an excellent resource.

## Managing Mail

The e-mail package I use (*Eudora Pro*) includes mailboxes and filters. "Mailboxes" hold messages according to themes I choose. *Eudora Pro* comes with three mailboxes: in, out, and trash. "In" holds all incoming messages not filtered to a mailbox. "Out" holds all outgoing messages temporarily, and retains copies of messages as I indicate. "Trash" holds those messages I want to discard; there is an option to retain those in trash or actually to discard them which appears at the end of a session. I can empty the trash at any time. All of the other 20+ mailboxes on my computer are of my own creation.

The filters I create sort my incoming into appropriate mailboxes. All messages not filtered end up in my "In" box. So, some very high-traffic listservs like ChemEd-L are sorted into a single place. When I leave town, I can either turn off a listserv or keep receiving as many as hundreds of messages that might arrive during a week — for reading or bulk discarding on my return.

I read about 10 listservs and 20 news groups regularly. Many topics that I find interesting come up on the ChemEd listserv. I read the HyperCard and Apple news groups. I've asked questions on all of these, and received very helpful responses. Also, I've provided answers to posted questions. In fact, I've stirred up a thing or two on the ChemEd list.

These days I spend much more time reading incoming information than I ever did 10 years ago, but I also spend less time in correspondence than before. On balance, I've devoted about 10 hours per week to electronic communications, and I'm not quite sure what I'm getting out of it. I think my work is broadening as a result, but I'm not sure this is true either. I *am certain* that my e-mail with students is effective.


## Discussion Group Software

As experienced WWW users might suspect, there are Web sites that specialize in disseminating information about discussion forums and related software. David Woolley maintains such a site [URL Q]. One can have all manners of software for all kinds of sites. The *NetForms* software impresses me [URL R]. You can visit the *NetForms* site and post something to see how this might work for a teacher. The educational price seems quite reasonable. After about 15 minutes of trying out the software, I ordered it for more extensive testing.

The next chapter deals with HTML forms, and HTML form elements. I think the teacher's goal ought to be to create a Web page that students access, enter their information, and submit to a server. At the server side, decisions are made about what to do with that information. Your teaching goal is to make contributed information WWW-accessible to your students in some fashion that is systematic enough to enhance their learning. There are many ways to accomplish this goal.

The WWW being what it is, several freeware and shareware alternatives have developed. One of my colleagues, Al Steckelberg, has used several of these to support a discussion group of paraprofessionals who are dispersed across Nebraska. As of this writing, he sees shortcomings in all such programs — each having desirable and undesirable features. John Orr, a UNL mathematician, has taught a senior/graduate-level course using a Web site as a focus for providing and sharing materials. He has developed software that facilitates discussion. It takes a student's response, automatically packages it as HTML at the end of related discussion, and posts it on Orr's server. Samples of this output were shown earlier in this chapter (p. 89). Notice that Orr posts his questions in the form of images so as to be able to present appropriate notation. This highlights a current limitation of discussion groups for the WWW, namely, specialized symbols present a significant problem that requires work-arounds.

Several people have developed software using *HyperCard* that works on supporting asynchronous discussion groups.

*Lotus Notes* is one program that you can use to handle discussion. Documents can be posted, and discussion added in such a way that the history of the discussion is maintained. *Notes* was an early example of groupware, software that enabled collaboration during document creation and editing. Several courses on my campus run using *Notes*; the history goes back to early 1995. The faculty users are extremely happy. In the earliest usage, students connected by modem to specific servers; they did not use the WWW. Current incarnations of *Notes* are made for Web use. The *Notes* server program is not available for Mac servers, however. *Notes* affords a very systematic, clean approach to sharing information and editing. It is also quite expensive. One important advantage to *Notes* is that the interface is that of a slick application rather than the somewhat inelegant appearance characteristic of an HTML form.

## Synchronous Discussion (Chatting)

There are two categories of discussion. When participants add commentary at different times, the discussion is asynchronous. In a synchronous discussion, everyone connects at the same time. *RoundTable* (Figure 8.4) is a multi-platform program that enables discussion groups. The client-side software currently is distributed without cost. The server software with unlimited users was listed at $8000 from which there was a substantial educational discount as *Web-Teaching* went to press. The company (ForeFront Group, www.ffg.com) describes *RoundTable* as follows: "The RoundTable meeting window is organized around three 'panes' — the Chat Panel, the Meeting Roster and the Canvas workspace. The Chat Panel is used for typing, sending and viewing text-based chat. The Meeting Roster displays the list of participants at the meeting. The Canvas provides a workspace for sharing multimedia information. Simply Drag and Drop or Cut/Copy and Paste images, documents, URLs, audio, video, or any file, into the canvas to share it with all participants in the meeting." At the time this book went to press, the server-side software was available only for Windows 95 and Windows NT systems.

Another recently released product for the Macintosh world is *ChitChat* by Mainstay software [URL V]. It appears to offer features similar to *RoundTable*. At press time, *ChitChat* was $495 for 50 users.

## VIDEOCONFERENCING

Soon to come on the WWW as an *everyday* technology are telephony and shared whiteboards. In telephony, the computer and WWW replace the telephone. This demands an entirely new way of thinking about the telephone. The providers may not be today's phone companies; cable TV and/or other providers may get into this act. For example, pricing is very unclear. Many Internet providers now charge $30 per month for unlimited connect time. If the lines are fast enough, why should I spend $60 per month with MCI to spend 100 minutes speaking with my daughter in Britain? Instead, she and I would just start an Internet-based connection. We would both talk and see one another. As bandwidth grows and hardware becomes disseminated, expect the importance of telephones to wane considerably.

In February 1997, as this book went to press, Texas Instruments announced an entirely new digital signal processor chip selling for less than $100 in quantity. This chip will decrease download times by factors of over 100 relative to the best of today's modems. As such quantum leap solutions to the bandwidth problem emerge, expect tasks like videoconferencing and the sharing of whiteboards to become even more commonplace than today's telephones.

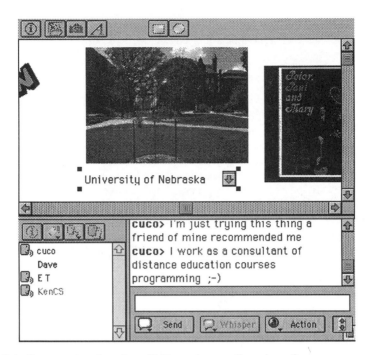

Figure 8.4. Screen capture from *RoundTable* synchronous discussion software.

Today you can purchase for under $100 a small, unobtrusive B&W video-camera that will sit atop your computer's monitor and record continuously (Figure 8.5). Freeware developed at Cornell University (*CU-SeeMe*) can be used to take that video and put it out to the Internet. If you know what the address of this source is, and you have appropriate software (*CU-SeeMe*), you can bring this up on your screen. That may not seem like too much, but it really is an innovation. The limitation, of course, is bandwidth. Both sender and receiver must be able to put lots of bits through their machines; the video and the sound take a great deal of memory. Also, that data stream moves over the Internet, and that's a big chunk of bandwidth being tied up, one that goes on in real time for the duration of the connection.

*CU-SeeMe* is audio/video conferencing software to connect one machine to another machine. Using a "reflector," you can connect one-to-many or many-to-many in a conference. We are developing a reflector site: reflector.unl.edu. A reflector behaves like a switchboard; all connected can watch one site, or there can be a many-sided conference. Expect to see this sort of software built into Web browsers soon.

By using *CU-SeeMe*, participants in a global environmental project for elementary school students were able to "appear" with the project's directors at a conference in late 1995 where they were giving a presentation about their work.

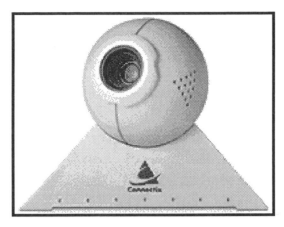

Figure 8.5. Connectix QuickCam. Put this unit on top of your monitor and, when connected with appropriate software in place, you are ready to broadcast your picture over the Internet.

Figure 8.6. Picture taken with low-cost B&W Connectix QuickCam. The screen display is from the Connectix *QuickMovie* software.

Project participants in one group were from Australia, South Africa, New Zealand, British Columbia, and two U.S. states. Through *CU-SeeMe*, teachers from New Zealand, Nebraska, and Texas were able to provide commentary on their involvement in the environmental project, as well as answer questions from the audience for those attending the conference in Florida.

*CU-SeeMe* allowed everyone involved to have clear audio continuously, and clear, live video, when needed. When one of the remote-site presenters was speaking, their video image was projected to the conference attendees, and a video image of the audience in attendance (a packed room) was relayed to the speaking presenter. When not speaking, presenters had a still video image of the session attendees on their computer screen together with continuous live audio. Two elementary students in Nebraska, as well as preservice teachers who were working in the lab, observed the *CU-SeeMe* session. All were engaged and delighted to be included.

Low-quality, Internet-based audiovisual communication, while far from perfect, is going to have a big impact on instruction. It is a very reasonable way to conduct many student–teacher conferences now held face to face. Faculty office hours can be quite different — arranged in advance by e-mail, and conducted from faculty home to student home.

My sense is that completely unsupervised courses with little teacher–student interaction have little prospect for success. After all, staring at a screen and clicking on the "blue" lines is little different than flipping through the pages of a book with photons being reflected from the page and presumably arriving at the eye but with no important neural processing whatsoever. The learner gains absolutely nothing.

While Web teleconferencing may not be as good as presence in a classroom or office, it is likely to afford enough of a personal interaction such that the teacher can provide adequate motivation and direction for the students. This is a guess. It may equal or surpass what can happen in a lecture setting; I suspect it won't match what is possible in a teaching laboratory. WWW teleconferencing may do even more. With just a bit more sophisticated camera and some higher resolution software, the quality of the transmitted images might enable supervision of lab work or collegial assistance with interpretation of real phenomena. The hardware and software commonly in use today usually are not quite up to the task, however. Nevertheless, most such tasks are a lot less technically challenging than, say, transmitting quality X rays for physician review.

My bias emerges again; I suspect this will not replace the press of the flesh that goes with the classroom. Also, there are some things I would never do over the Internet — like tell a student that his graduate work wasn't cutting it, and that he was being terminated from a program. When a reviewer challenged this notion with "Why not?" I still felt this was something I wouldn't do.

I do see other positive changes, however. For example, I envision small groups of three or four students working at a terminal being encouraged and led by a faculty member at a distant site. The small-group work that I've required has often been a problem since graduate students may travel from far away and find scheduling time with one another difficult. I see electronic conferencing within student groups as a strategy for enabling student collaboration. Perhaps *some* laboratory work can be supervised this way.

Several tutorial centers on my campus hold late evening hours. Scheduling these always is a challenge. Also, there is a substantial perceived safety risk involved for late evening walks on campus. One can envision such tutoring being conducted between a teaching assistant's apartment or home and a student's dormitory or home via Web-conferencing.

Some courses I teach demand discussion. *Much* instructional design is a matter of opinion rather than science, and a class of 15 students is likely to include skilled, experienced participants with opposing views. Developing those contrasts is what I try to accomplish during class meetings. I'm beginning to think I should try this on the Web.

Other courses I teach require little discussion. I don't care what your opinion is about HTML tags and how they work, for example. The look of a Web page and how one interacts with it is an open-ended design issue, however, where evaluative boundaries are soft. I'm perfectly happy to teach the how-to courses on the Web, but still believe that those issues demanding judgment and discussion be dealt with face to face. (Face validity may be a disease.)

## TELEPHONY; SHARED WHITEBOARDS

As noted earlier, the Web is likely to replace the telephone, or at least change typical telephone use drastically. A whiteboard that users at both ends of a live conversation may mark can be included (Figure 8.7). One user might mark with blue and the other green, for example.

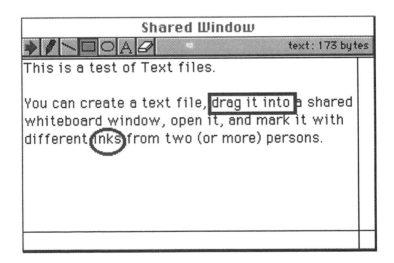

Figure 8.7.  Screen capture from shared whiteboard.

Expect conversations and shared whiteboards to play a large role in teaching, especially for individual conferences and office hours (Figure 8.8).

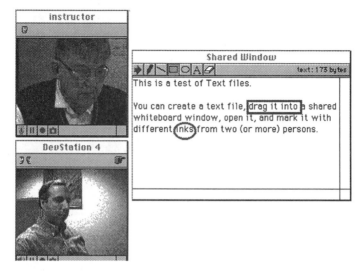

Figure 8.8.  Whiteboard shown with images of persons at either end where both video and audio connections also are in place.  Dave Bentz, lower left, is a UNL telecommunications expert.

# CHAPTER 9

# INTERACTIVE STRATEGIES; FORMS

This chapter concerns the creation of interactive environments between students and/or the teacher using the WWW. By using questioning and other techniques in your classroom, you can elicit responses and give feedback on a time scale measured in seconds or minutes. Each student can be called on, and you can question in such a way that nearly all students are always prepared to respond. If you use cooperative strategies, you might even be successful at utilizing more questioning to get higher overall response rates. At first blush, active learning might seem to be easy to achieve in a classroom. As the teacher, you can ask questions. Sometimes your glances or gestures can evoke significant student participation. Again, research tends to support the notion that teacher questions are less effective than teachers think, and that most teacher-centered classrooms do not involve as much active learning as the opening lines of this chapter might suggest. The tasks that the teacher sets for the students usually determine the extent of active learning. This chapter has the twofold purpose found else-where in this book. One dimension has you focusing on the nature of the task of creating active learning environments, and the other on the tools available to help you to accomplish that task.

The clear exposition of information with multimedia and hyperlinked text and nearly 168 hour per week accessibility is a reality when using the WWW. After some thoughtful design, you can accomplish the delivery of the material of a traditional lecture using the WWW (see p. ix). Your future efforts can be aimed at upgrading content and keeping it current, and seeking out multimedia materials of ever increasing quality. In spite of often-heard complaints, students *do* learn from lectures. Lecturing certainly was the primary means of instruction when I went to college and graduate school — even high school. Self-regulating learners perform well in just about any learning environment. For example, chemistry seminars and colloquia at major research universities focus on new works and discoveries in colloquia. The faculty usually have a keen interest in the subject, and attend with little external motivation. They, in turn, devise teaching strategies for increasing graduate student participation. One "motivational" strategy involves including material from seminars and colloquia on cumulative exams required of predoctoral candidates.

I've heard it argued by persons who teach and perform research in self-regulation that lectures work well for poor self-regulators. During class, the lecturer can drop survival hints, strategies, and other clues that help the poor self-regulators survive. The point here may well be that if students don't show up in class, they may have no source of such information.

Experienced teachers know, however, that many books provide seemingly clear expositions of content and, in spite of round-the-clock access to those books, student learning is less than desired. As noted many times in this book, research suggests that efficient learning requires active learners. As a teacher, you get to create and employ those strategies that make learning active. With your students sitting in front of tubes somewhere on the WWW, how do you create an interactive environment for them? My view at this time about the instructional materials likely to emerge in tidal waves on the WWW is that most will be lacking in interactivity.

## HYPERTEXT LINKS

Hypertext is readily achieved within WWW documents.

Hypertext is nonlinear, or nonsequential text. That is, the text organized so you can easily jump around from topic to topic. You do not need to read the text in a fixed sequence. Although hypertext is probably best brought to life on a computer, you can find hypertext in simple paper documents.

Seyer, 1991, p. 1

Hypertext requires readers to make decisions about their reading. To this degree, it is an active learning strategy. My own interest in this area started when I first learned *HyperCard*, a multimedia computer application developed for Macintosh computers and first released in August 1987. *HyperCard* was an excellent way to create "two screen" videodisk programs, and that was my principal interest at the time. In fact, *HyperCard* is a rather powerful programming tool that one can use to accomplish many tasks of which creating hypertext is but one. Making choices often appears on lists of ways to create active learning environments. Hypertext links empower choice and, therefore, are potentially valuable instructional tools.

In this book, the definition of hypertext was included in the linear text. It stood out on a light gray background. You could have skipped over reading it, but you probably didn't. In a WWW document, the word *hypertext* could have been made to appear as a link. Links are identified by being both underlined and set with type in a different color. WWW browser software keeps track of the links you've used and, if you've visited the link recently, it appears in still a different color. [In *HyperCard*, links need not be identified; also, the user could come across a term and find no link. With *HyperCard*, the user can think that a link is appropriate (i.e., think it should be there) and click repeatedly with no effect.]

There is a design issue with hypertext. As the designer, you must decide where a link would be appropriate and *you must put it there*. Some people think the computer ought to be able to do that for us automatically. While perhaps a noble goal, that requires a level of artificial intelligence not usually a part of learning materials.

There is a design issue about the use of click here, for example. Since hypertext links appear with a characteristic color and nearly always underlined, the need for an instruction is diminished. For frequent users of the Web, click here is superfluous. So, if you see David W. Brooks in a WWW document, you can assume that clicking that will bring up information about Brooks. I prefer to use a statement like "Send e-mail to David W. Brooks, dbrooks1@unl.edu" to indicate e-mailing. A user can copy the e-mail address to some other file for a different purpose than intended in the Web document.

If there is a hypertext link in your materials, *it is because you put it there*. Deciding which links may be appropriate, when to create materials yourself and when to send students out on the WWW to find information, and deciding how to get students back all are instructional design issues. Should you try to devise a way to determine how many links your students visit?

One of my most creative colleagues works for the National Arbor Day Foundation. She once developed a *HyperCard*-based version of a 'tree key.' This key actually consists of a series of questions one asks about the attributes of the leaves and bark of a tree such that, after just a few questions, the tree can be uniquely identified — so that it can be labeled as a *silver maple* or a *thornless locust*. This is a problem very well suited for *HyperCard*, and converting it to a WWW format is straightforward. Indeed, rich drawings and photographs about the questions can appear as clickable entities on the WWW with one question leading to the next until the final page visited gives the name of the tree with its picture.

In the HTML document specifications currently available, one easily can make an entire image a clickable entity. By placing a border around the image, the size of which alerts the user and the color of which conveys the property of "clickability," attractive hypertext "keys" are created readily (Figure 9.1).

The tree key is an example of how one might use hypertext links in a meaningful and instructive way. While carrying WWW client software into the woods is problematic, having students gather leaf and sometimes bark samples for the classroom is a time-honored approach to this sort of learning. It is possible to see how this could be developed as a very powerful resource, one that could go far beyond traditional paper texts. At this time, WWW-based tree keys are no market threat to the pocket-sized books one carries off to the woods.

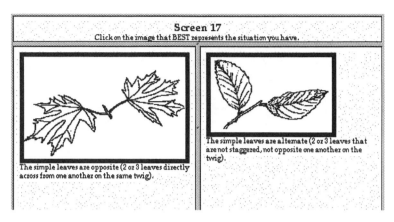

Figure 9.1. Sample of tree key, taken from an early project by Mimi Wickless. Imagine how attractive this might look in color with built-in hypertext tutoring!

It is very easy to see how they could be made into a powerful classroom teaching enhancement, however.

What kinds of materials are well suited for the WWW? Somewhere in the back of my brain is the fact that a videodisk was made with duplications of X rays for about 300 different kinds of breast tumors. I can see this used in WWW-based problems approached via hypertext links. If I were teaching art or architecture, it would seem to me that opportunities for linking would abound. Indeed, a very large number of the projects my students have developed over the years could readily be ported to WWW formats and retain essentially all of their interactivity.

Recall the earlier comments of Schwartz [1995] about the voice of the author: you'll need some way to bring the students back to the track you've created if following that track is, indeed, some sort of curriculum goal.


## MAPS

In HTML jargon, a map is an image that has clickable hot spots. So, a map makes it possible to have just a part of an image interactive, or to have different parts of images interact in different ways. This technique also is readily accomplished by essentially all of the hypermedia programs currently available (e.g., *Toolbook*, *HyperCard*).

When you're on the WWW and see some large graphic that seems to say "click me," that probably was developed as a map. When the cursor changes from a pointing arrow to a hand, a link is implied (Figure 9.2).

The user is supposed to have garnered enough WWW experience to know to click and, with the passage of time, that expectation becomes a reality. If

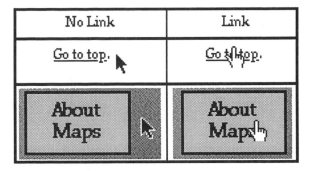

Figure 9.2. The arrow cursor on the left suggests no link; the hand cursor on the right suggests a link, and that clicking will bring about some action — going someplace implied by the image or text.

you've been on the WWW often, you can bet that you've interacted with a map.

### Client-Side Maps

Technically speaking, there are two different ways to develop maps. One involves HTML code that is used by the client. Several new browsers make use of client-side maps. In this code, rectangles defining clickable areas are specified in terms of pixel coordinates in the image. The only thing special about the image is that the tag for the image will contain the attribute USEMAP. This allows the teacher to specify one or several rectangles in the image such that clicking within that rectangle will activate a link (URL) (Figure 9.3). Expressed in the simplest way, teachers can create hypertext links within images.

Advantages accrue to using client-side maps. First, you don't need to go back to the server to interpret the click; once the document is at the client, you need go no further. This is particularly helpful when the links are to places within the same document. Another advantage is that you don't have to create files for the server enabling it to interpret user clicks. In other words, you can minimize your dependence on the server.

Shareware software packages are available to help the designer locate rectangles within images, and to write the necessary HTML code.

### Server-Side Maps

Server-side maps are signified by including the word ISMAP in the tag for the image. Without providing details, this affords interactivity to parts of an image. You must return to the server, however, even if you are just going to a location within the current document. This is a serious time constraint, especially when dealing with limited bandwidth.

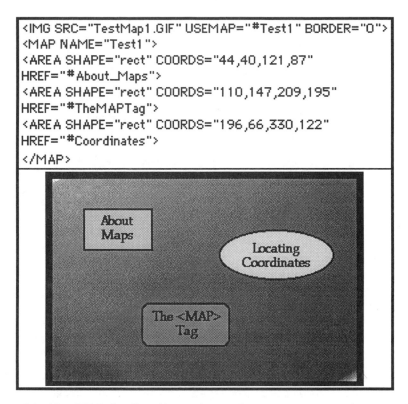

```
<IMG SRC="TestMap1.GIF" USEMAP="#Test1" BORDER="0">
<MAP NAME="Test1">
<AREA SHAPE="rect" COORDS="44,40,121,87"
HREF="#About_Maps">
<AREA SHAPE="rect" COORDS="110,147,209,195"
HREF="#TheMAPTag">
<AREA SHAPE="rect" COORDS="196,66,330,122"
HREF="#Coordinates">
</MAP>
```

Figure 9.3. Top, HTML for client-side map image. Bottom, screen capture of corresponding client-side map.

"Hot spots" other than rectangles can be defined including circles, points, and polygons on server-side maps. If your intent is to serve out a new document rather than move within a document, then the potential bandwidth problem is not so serious. You might already have guessed that I advocate client-side maps in any case. Keep the traffic to a server as low as possible. *Never* squander bandwidth.

## KEEPING TRACK OF HYPERTEXT MOVES

In *HyperCard* and most of the other powerful hypermedia programs, it is a rather straightforward matter to develop strategies that keep track of student choices. You can see which links a student visits, and record the amount of time spent here and there. This is also done easily and in a manner that is largely transparent to the students. (No fair if you don't tell the student up-front when you are doing this, and "dirty pool" if you count this in some way without telling them! It is, nevertheless, a gold mine for those in search of doctoral degrees in education topics.)

When students are in a student lab using institutional hardware, a monitor or proctor might be able to make some judgment about the degree to which they remain "on task." While one of the advantages of WWW instruction is "any time, any place," a corresponding disadvantage is the difficulty of documenting either effort or performance. (Sometimes making effective choices with links is a mark of high learning.)

So far as I know, there is no easy way to get an indication of time on task for students using the WWW. But, as of this writing, the student must connect to the server before some student-specific record can be made. While it is easy to see how you could deal with this problem — say have students log into a database at the start of a WWW session, and then make some brief report at the conclusion of the session describing their travels — the inability to perform any kind of serious tracking seems to be a disadvantage of WWW-based instruction. I expect this problem to be solved soon using either scripting or programming. The solution may involve passing and storing **cookies\*** (small amounts of persistent information) between server and client or among appropriately scripted pages.

## FORMS

While hypertext links afford some very large degree of interactivity, clicking without a purpose is possible and verification is not easily achieved. Most teachers want some feedback from students that shows more learning than just making a series of choices. This brings us to the form element of HTML. Forms are not a simple matter. You must decide how you will gather and use the information obtained from a form. The simplest procedure is to have that information e-mailed either to you or to some grader or recorder. A more complex way is to have the information from a form processed automatically by the server. That choice today still means programming. It can be simple, copycat programming, but it is programming nevertheless. I discuss form input elements first, followed by what to do with the input. The variety of form input elements is increasing. As new types are added, the power of this method increases. Gaps remain. It is not a simple matter to input voice or to capture a simple sketch created by the learner.

## TEXT

The TEXT element affords an open-ended, free-form response from a learner. It is equivalent to what teachers might call a short-answer response in a quiz. TEXT can be used to obtain the student's name, address, and other personal or demographic information.

```
<FORM>
<B>Enter Address:</B>
<INPUT TYPE="text" NAME="Address"
VALUE="Your Home Address"  SIZE=30 MAXLENGTH=28>
</FORM>
```

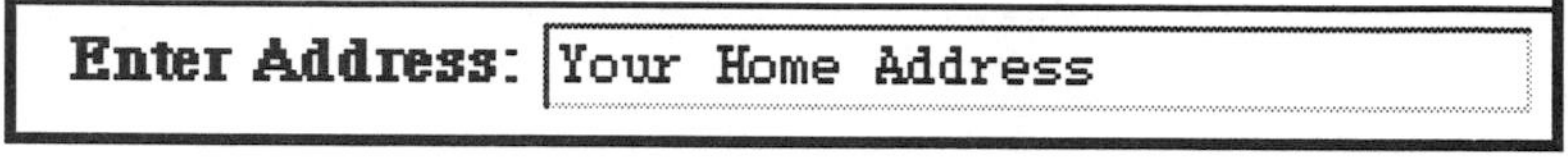

**Enter Address:** | Your Home Address

Figure 9.4. Top, HTML for creating a TEXT element in a form. Bottom, screen capture of that TEXT element in form.

The TEXT input element has much potential for teachers. For example, if a student should be able to perform a calculation, then this might be the way to get feedback about the result.

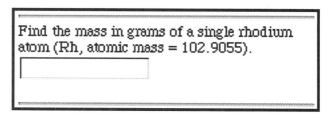

Find the mass in grams of a single rhodium atom (Rh, atomic mass = 102.9055).

Figure 9.5. Screen capture of a TEXT element in quiz form.

The question information can include media information. You can have short-answer questions with accompanying figures or movies, for example (Figure 9.6).

## PASSWORD

PASSWORD is similar to text except that the typed characters are encoded into large dots so that persons watching the screen cannot tell which characters have been typed (Figure 9.7). As its name implies, the most common use of this input element is for entering passwords. One can imagine variations such as having two or three students work together in a group where the responses are kept secure from one another in some kind of gaming strategy, for example.

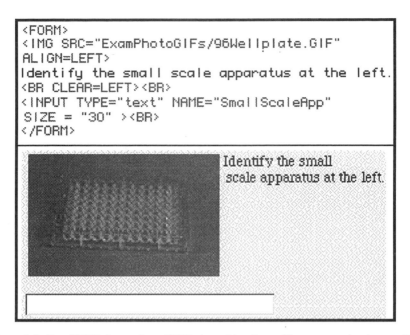

```
<FORM>
<IMG SRC="ExamPhotoGIFs/96Wellplate.GIF"
ALIGN=LEFT>
Identify the small scale apparatus at the left.
<BR CLEAR=LEFT><BR>
<INPUT TYPE="text" NAME="SmallScaleApp"
SIZE = "30" ><BR>
</FORM>
```

Figure 9.6.  Top, HTML for creating a TEXT element in a form with accompanying image.  Bottom, screen capture of that TEXT element in form.  Note the image above the text entry field.

```
<FORM>
<B>Enter Password:</B>
<INPUT TYPE="password" NAME="PassWd">
</FORM>
```

| **Enter Password:** |  |
|---|---|
| **Enter Password:** | ●●●●● |

Figure 9.7.  Top, HTML for creating a PASSWORD element in a form.  Bottom, screen capture of that PASSWORD element in form, first blank, and then filled in.

## CHECKBOX

A CHECKBOX element allows a simple indication of yes/no or true/false for some circumstances where the outcome of the choice does not preclude other choices.  So, for example, when ordering a hamburger one might have an order that looks something like Figure 9.8.

```
<FORM>
<B>Hamburger Order</B><P>
<INPUT TYPE="radio" NAME="Bun" VALUE="White"
CHECKED>  White
<INPUT TYPE="radio" NAME="Bun" VALUE="WholeWheat">
Whole Wheat<P>
<INPUT TYPE="checkbox" NAME="Cheese" VALUE="ON">
Cheese<BR>
<INPUT TYPE="checkbox" NAME="Mustard" VALUE="ON">
Mustard<BR>
<INPUT TYPE="checkbox" NAME="Catsup" VALUE="ON">
Catsup<BR>
<INPUT TYPE="checkbox" NAME="Mayo" VALUE="ON">
Mayo<BR>
<INPUT TYPE="checkbox" NAME="Tomato" VALUE="ON">
Tomato<BR>
<INPUT TYPE="checkbox" NAME="Lettuce" VALUE="ON">
Lettuce<BR>
<INPUT TYPE="checkbox" NAME="Onion" VALUE="ON">
Onion<BR>
</FORM>
```

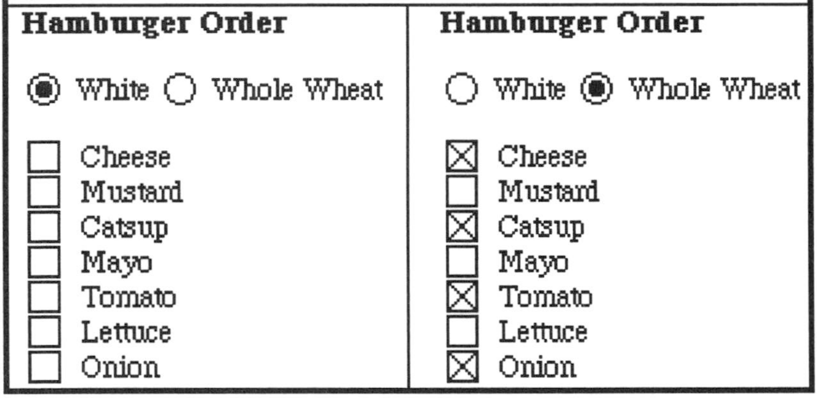

| **Hamburger Order** | **Hamburger Order** |
| --- | --- |
| ⦿ White ○ Whole Wheat | ○ White ⦿ Whole Wheat |
| ☐ Cheese | ☒ Cheese |
| ☐ Mustard | ☐ Mustard |
| ☐ Catsup | ☒ Catsup |
| ☐ Mayo | ☐ Mayo |
| ☐ Tomato | ☒ Tomato |
| ☐ Lettuce | ☐ Lettuce |
| ☐ Onion | ☒ Onion |

Figure 9.8. Top, HTML for creating a text entry in a form with several CHECKBOX elements. Bottom, screen capture of those CHECKBOX elements in form.

This could be included into a more typical exam-type situation (Figure 9.9).

> Question 7. Which items of safety
> gear should be used when handling
> concentrated sulfuric acid in 50-mL
> amounts?
>
> ☐ splash goggles
> ☒ face shield
> ☒ apron
> ☐ lab coat
> ☒ rubber gloves
>
> ( Send in Quiz Answers )

Figure 9.9.  Using CHECKBOX items for a multiple-choice test.

## RADIO

A RADIO button behaves the same way as a CHECKBOX except that the choices to be made must be mutually exclusive.  That is, checking one of the boxes precludes checking some other button in the family.  A straightforward example is that of male/female where the choices are regarded as mutually exclusive (Figure 9.10).

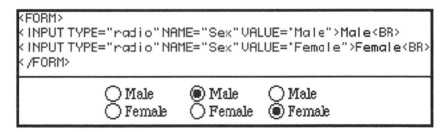

```
<FORM>
< INPUT TYPE="radio" NAME="Sex" VALUE="Male">Male<BR>
< INPUT TYPE="radio" NAME="Sex" VALUE="Female">Female<BR>
< /FORM>
```

Figure 9.10.  Top, HTML for creating a radio button entry in a form.  Bottom, screen capture of that radio button entry in form, first blank, and then filled in.  Clicking "Female" in the middle example brings up the right-hand example, with "Female" on and "Male" off.

One of the buttons can be set "on" when the page appears.  Clicking any one of these buttons causes any other button with the same name to be turned off.  RADIO buttons offer one way to accomplish a multiple-choice test (Figure 9.11).

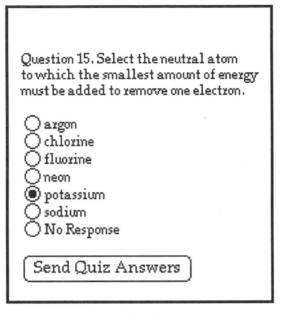

**Figure 9.11**. Using RADIO buttons for a multiple-choice test.

## SELECT

SELECT is a form element with a menu-style choice. One must intuitively move the cursor over the "select" bar, press, and drag to the desired choice, releasing once the choice is made. There are no clues about using this form input element; again, experienced users have encountered them more than once (Figure 9.12).

This input strategy could be used as easily as any for using radio buttons in multiple-choice situations. So, instead of having a list of majors, you could have a list of answers. You also can set a default item, an item that comes up checked. In Figure 9.12 we chose chemistry as the default item.

Unlike RADIO buttons, SELECT can be set to accept multiple selections. Again, one needs somehow to know that holding the Command-Key down and clicking a choice turns that particular choice on or off independent of others making multiple selections possible (Figure 9.13).

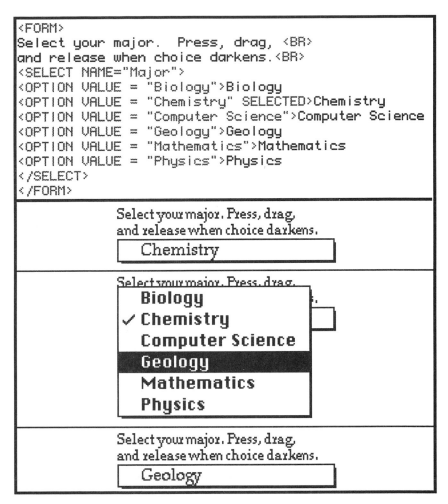

```
<FORM>
Select your major.  Press, drag, <BR>
and release when choice darkens.<BR>
<SELECT NAME="Major">
<OPTION VALUE = "Biology">Biology
<OPTION VALUE = "Chemistry" SELECTED>Chemistry
<OPTION VALUE = "Computer Science">Computer Science
<OPTION VALUE = "Geology">Geology
<OPTION VALUE = "Mathematics">Mathematics
<OPTION VALUE = "Physics">Physics
</SELECT>
</FORM>
```

Select your major. Press, drag,
and release when choice darkens.

| Chemistry |

Select your major. Press, drag,

**Biology**
✓ **Chemistry**
**Computer Science**
**Geology**
**Mathematics**
**Physics**

Select your major. Press, drag,
and release when choice darkens.

| Geology |

**Figure 9.12**. The SELECT form element permits selection from a pop-up list of choices. One of the choices can be made the default choice by labeling it SELECTED in the HTML. Top, HTML for the select element in the form. Second, screen capture as it first appears. Third, appearance when pressed and dragged to choose "Geology." Bottom, screen capture after "Geology" selected.

## HIDDEN

The HIDDEN input element affords some real power to the teacher. In the on-line chemistry test we developed to demonstrate WWW interactivity, the starting point asked the user to enter his or her name. Once this was entered by the user and submitted in one item of a form, all of the subsequent documents (which consisted of exams and exams with answers) identified the user by name.

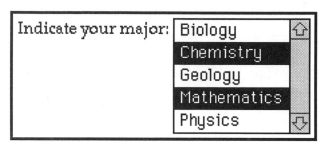

Figure 9.13. Screen capture of SELECT form element when button is pressed and two items have been chosen.

This was accomplished by incorporating the name in each subsequent document as a HIDDEN input element. This information was made available to the program that performed the exam generating or evaluating tasks (Figure 9.14).

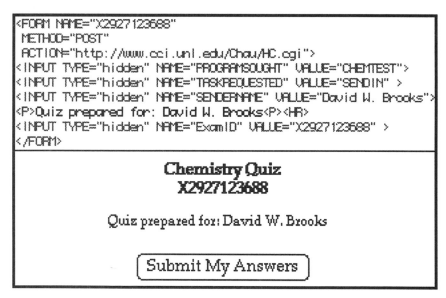

Figure 9.14. Uses of the HIDDEN form element in coding exams. Top, the four HIDDEN elements will be transferred with other form entries when the form is submitted. The form has been set up so that, as shown in the screen capture at the bottom, two of the four HIDDEN items also were shown directly in the form at the client side. The HIDDEN items, however, and not those visible are submitted with the form inputs.

Another HIDDEN input was used to label exams. Because anyone could take the chemistry test anywhere in the world, there needed to be a way to label uniquely each exam that was created. This was accomplished using the time feature in the exam software. Macintoshes keep track of time beginning at midnight, January 1, 1904. One system value that Macs have available is the number of seconds that have elapsed since that moment in time. So, the number of seconds becomes a unique and therefore identifying number when used in a computer program that takes more than 1 second to generate a chemistry exam. So, each exam created was labeled with the string consisting of the letter "X" followed by the time, in seconds, since midnight, 1/1/04, when the exam was created. This label was carried in the exam document as a HIDDEN input element.

## SUBMIT

SUBMIT is a form input element required to tell the browser software when the user thinks the form is complete and should be submitted for processing. This is a purely mechanical thing, but one that deserves attention. Submitting answers that a learner has added to a form is a key feature of interactivity. In the absence of some scripting or Java application, there is no way for the server to poll the client, nor is there a way for the client to send some preview of the information being created to the server. As the teacher, you do have one option with respect to the submit button, namely, to determine what the button actually says (Figure 9.15).

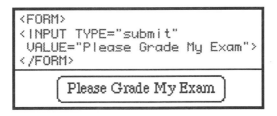

Figure 9.15. Top, HTML for creating a SUBMIT button on a form. Bottom, screen capture of that button. Be explicit about the wording used for the button; have it serve your purpose.

## RESET

RESET creates a button that empties *all* of the form inputs except HIDDEN, and resets any preselected choices to their default values. This provides an action for cleaning up. Most of the time, the user is sent a form fresh from the server, and never gets to use this button. Besides, it is a rather dramatic event, since *all* of the entered information is erased. Most users would usually prefer to erase just one or a few items in a large form. Again, the teacher can add special text for this button. When choosing text, it is better to be informative than cute (Figure 9.16).

```
<FORM>
<INPUT TYPE="reset" VALUE="Erase My Entries">
</FORM>
```

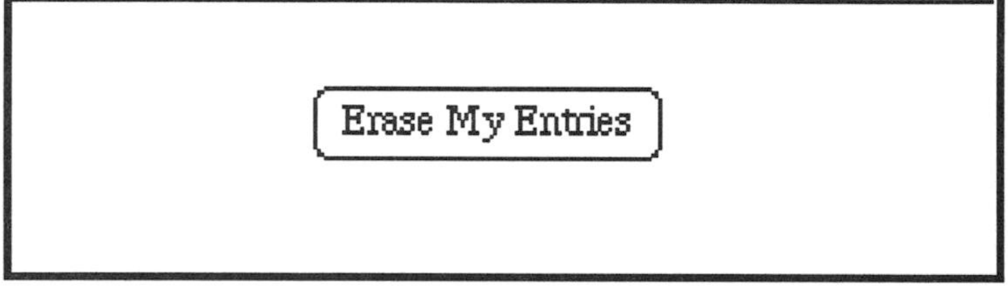

```
[ Erase My Entries ]
```

Figure 9.16. Top, HTML for creating a RESET button on a form. Bottom, screen capture of that button. Be explicit about the wording used for the button; have it serve your purpose.

## TEXTAREA

The TEXTAREA input element permits learners to write a great deal of text for inclusion in their response. This is where a student might be asked to write one or several paragraphs (Figure 9.17).

As of this writing, it is exceptionally unlikely that you will have or be able to create software tools that will adequately judge the quality of a lengthy student response. For that reason, you'll probably be reading all of this material yourself, or directing it to some grader or reader.

## COLLECTING STUDENT TEXT

If lengthy responses are intended, consider alternatives to forms and TEXTAREA. One alternative is to employ some common word processor (or a predetermined group of word processors), and have students create documents using that software. They can then attach the document to electronic mail to you. Modern e-mail software (such as *Eudora Pro*) handles attached documents readily. This seems to me to be a very much more reasonable way to go, since the student is free to enhance the document with pictures (and other multimedia).

The work of David Hibler, a colleague in the University of Nebraska English Department, was described earlier (p. 90). He has students create documents (with folders of accompanying images and multimedia) and tag these for HTML. Then these documents can become a part of his course. The strategy of having students publish their work increases the stakes for the students. When the stakes are raised, generally both the extent and quality of learning increase.

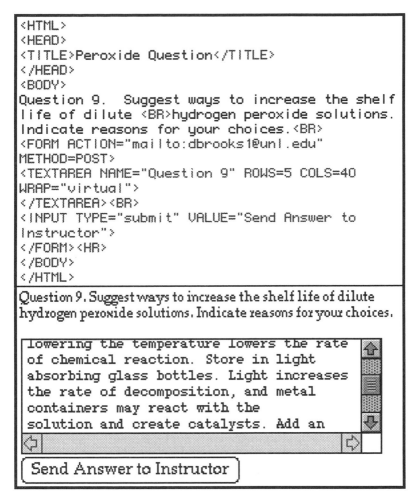

```
<HTML>
<HEAD>
<TITLE>Peroxide Question</TITLE>
</HEAD>
<BODY>
Question 9.  Suggest ways to increase the shelf
life of dilute <BR>hydrogen peroxide solutions.
Indicate reasons for your choices.<BR>
<FORM ACTION="mailto:dbrooks1@unl.edu"
METHOD=POST>
<TEXTAREA NAME="Question 9" ROWS=5 COLS=40
WRAP="virtual">
</TEXTAREA><BR>
<INPUT TYPE="submit" VALUE="Send Answer to
Instructor">
</FORM><HR>
</BODY>
</HTML>
```

Question 9. Suggest ways to increase the shelf life of dilute
hydrogen peroxide solutions. Indicate reasons for your choices.

```
lowering the temperature lowers the rate
of chemical reaction. Store in light
absorbing glass bottles. Light increases
the rate of decomposition, and metal
containers may react with the
solution and create catalysts. Add an
```

Send Answer to Instructor

Figure 9.17. Top, HTML for introducing TEXTAREA element in a form. Bottom, screen capture of that element after it has been filled in. Students can send large amounts of material to you for evaluation. This information can be directed toward your e-mail. By adding the attribute WRAP="virtual" to the TEXTAREA element, the information typed by the student will **wrap***
automatically on their screen in newer browsers.

## E-MAIL (FOR PROCESSING FORMS)

Form processing by e-mail may prove so helpful in getting you started that I considered devoting a separate short chapter to it. One of the easiest things you can do with the information gathered from a form is to have it e-mailed to your account (or some other specified account) (Figures 9.18, 9.19).

```
<HTML>
<HEAD>
<TITLE>Sample Form for E-Mail</TITLE>
</HEAD>
<BODY>
<H3 ALIGN=CENTER>Sample Form</H3><HR>
<FORM METHOD=POST ACTION="mailto:dbrooks1@unl.edu" >
The following is a text box.  It allows students to type conveniently
a string of characters.<P>
Please enter your name:
<INPUT TYPE="text" NAME="Name" SIZE=30 MAXLENGTH=28 VALUE="Jane/John
Doe"><P>
An equivalent entry is the Password input.<BR>
Please enter your password:
<INPUT TYPE="password" NAME="Password" SIZE=12 MAXLENGTH=10><P>
The following is a series of Radio Buttons.  These are mutually
exclusive.  <BR>
<INPUT TYPE="radio" NAME="Sex" VALUE="Male">Male<BR>
<INPUT TYPE="radio" NAME="Sex" VALUE="Female">Female<P>
The following is a series of check boxes.  These are not mutually
exclusive.  <BR>
<INPUT TYPE="checkbox" NAME="Mustard" VALUE="ON">Mustard?
<INPUT TYPE="checkbox" NAME="Tomato" VALUE="ON">Tomato?
<INPUT TYPE="checkbox" NAME="Pickles" VALUE="ON">Pickles? <P>
Students can enter large amounts of text.<BR>
Write a few sentences on the theme, Why I love Nebraska?<BR>
<TEXTAREA NAME="Why I love Nebraska" ROWS=5 COLS=60 WRAP="virtual" >
</TEXTAREA><P>
When pressed, select produces a menu from which a rainbow of
choices<BR> (ROYGBIV) can be made.<BR>
Press and choose your favorite color:<BR>
<SELECT NAME="Rainbow color">
<OPTION SELECTED>Red <OPTION >Orange <OPTION >Yellow <OPTION >Green
<OPTION >Blue <OPTION > Indigo <OPTION >Violet
</SELECT><P>
You can hide information in the form that is transmitted with the
form.  I've hidden my name.<P>
<INPUT TYPE="hidden" NAME="Hidden Information" VALUE="David W.
Brooks">
You can reset (ERASE) all form entries with a single click from a
reset button.<BR>
<INPUT TYPE="reset" VALUE="ERASE All Entries"><P>
You can mail the results with a submit button:<BR>
<INPUT TYPE="submit" VALUE="Mail these inputs to DWB">
</FORM>
<HR>
</BODY>
```

Figure 9.18.  Sample form HTML.

Although not the most interactive way to handle this situation (using a **cgi\*** has the potential to provide nearly instantaneous, on-demand feedback), it probably beats any conventional approach to either testing or grading homework.  You don't need some server software to process the form input.  You define an AC-TION for the form input.  By writing 'mailto:' followed by your e-mail address, the information comes to you.  Using this in a form tag will have e-mail sent to me:

```
<FORM METHOD="POST" ACTION="mailto:dbrooks1@unl.edu" >
```

What actually comes to your mail, however, is encoded and needs some decoding before you can make sense of it.  The data come in as one large string in which all spaces have been replaced by "+" (plus signs), and plus signs replaced by a code for plus signs (%2B).  For example, the form shown in

Figure 9.9 will e-mail the response "face+shield=chosen&apron
=chosen&rubber+gloves=chosen," while that from Figure 9.11 sends
"Question+15=potassium." A generic Macintosh program, *Mailto
Tamer*, will decode the mailed information for you (Figure 9.20).

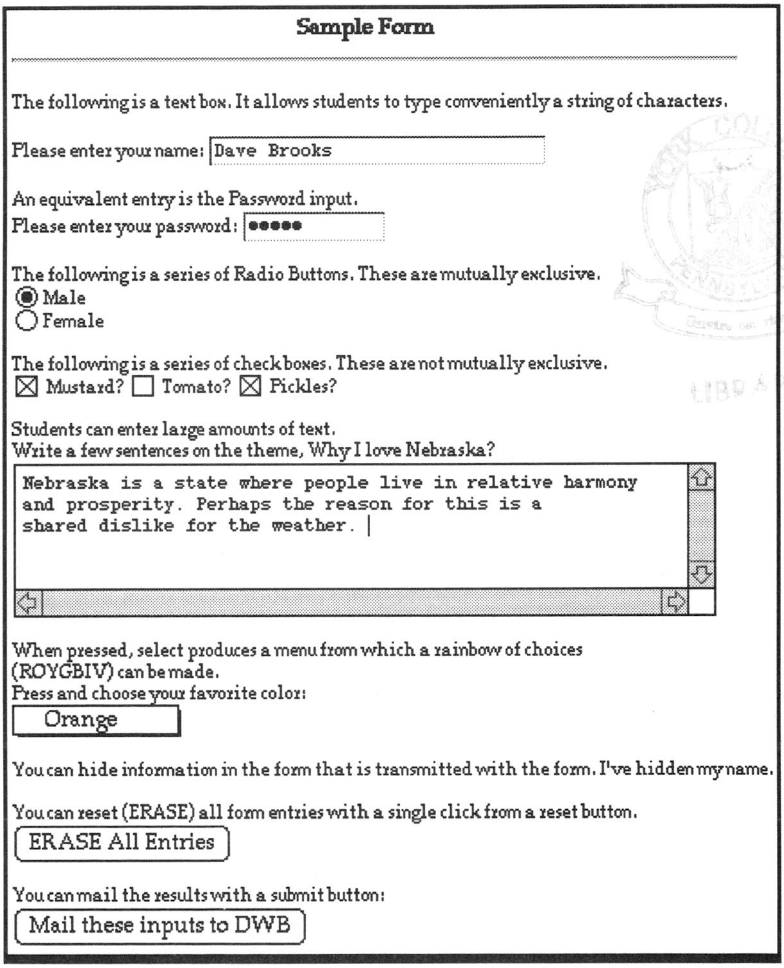

---

**Sample Form**

The following is a text box. It allows students to type conveniently a string of characters.

Please enter your name: | Dave Brooks |

An equivalent entry is the Password input.
Please enter your password: | ●●●●● |

The following is a series of Radio Buttons. These are mutually exclusive.
⦿ Male
◯ Female

The following is a series of checkboxes. These are not mutually exclusive.
☒ Mustard? ☐ Tomato? ☒ Pickles?

Students can enter large amounts of text.
Write a few sentences on the theme, Why I love Nebraska?

```
Nebraska is a state where people live in relative harmony
and prosperity. Perhaps the reason for this is a
shared dislike for the weather. |
```

When pressed, select produces a menu from which a rainbow of choices
(ROYGBIV) can be made.
Press and choose your favorite color:
| Orange |

You can hide information in the form that is transmitted with the form. I've hidden my name.

You can reset (ERASE) all form entries with a single click from a reset button.
[ ERASE All Entries ]

You can mail the results with a submit button:
[ Mail these inputs to DWB ]

---

Figure 9.19. Sample form created from HTML in Figure 9.18 as it appears in client browser.
This form solicits input from the learner.

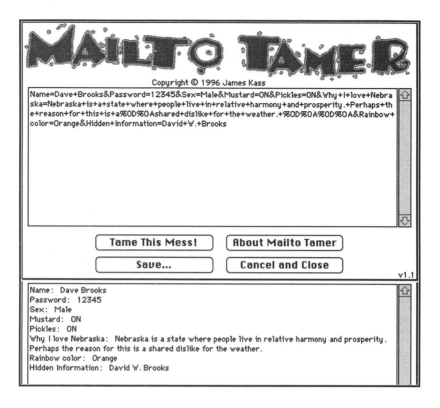

Figure 9.20. Sample of e-mail received from use of the form in Figure 9.19. Note the unusual encoding at the top, and the decoded version displayed at the bottom.

## SELECTED PROGRAMS

There are many interactive programs available today, and it seems that at least some attention has been addressed to making each one of them deliverable over the WWW.

### HyperCard

*HyperCard* is a powerful multimedia program. *Stoichiometer* [Brooks, 1994a, b], a program that takes formulas and numbers inputted by users to solve nearly all kinds of chemical bookkeeping problems, also stores variables that can be used to create tutoring in the form of worked-out examples. In other words, it computes context-specific tutoring. Although creating *Stoichiometer* was accomplished readily with *HyperCard*, it would have been a much more difficult task with any other tool or language. *HyperCard* handles color poorly. *Hyper-*

*Card* is Macintosh only. *HyperCard* can be extended with code added in the form of so-called XCMDs (X-commands). XCMDs are small portions of compiled code that *HyperCard* can use to enhance or extend its performance.

At the time of this writing, a product called *LiveCard* [URL T] emerged that purports to make existing stacks run over the WWW. *LiveCard* definitely has promise. Since *HyperCard* program (stacks) can take in information, many existing interactive programs might be made Web-ready in a brief time.

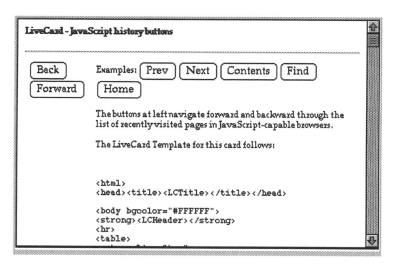

Figure 9.21. *HyperCard* playing over Web using *LiveCard*. This is a screen capture of a "stack" dealing with JavaScripts that is accessible from the Royal Software *LiveCard* address. [URL AG]

## SuperCard

*SuperCard* is a program very much like *HyperCard*. It handles color quite well, and has other attractive features relative to *HyperCard*. If the history of *HyperCard* has been complicated, then that of *SuperCard* is even more complicated. *SuperCard* recently was moved to Allegiant Technologies.

*SuperCard* is Macintosh only. A "*Windows*" player version of *Super-Card* was promised beginning in January 1995, but it has not emerged. The company's Web site showed "under construction" fully 2 years after the product was announced (and an alpha version demonstrated.) In January 1996, Allegiant introduced a series of XCMDs intended for Internet functions under the name *Marionet*.

Recently, a *SuperCard* WWW strategy was announced in the form of a plug-in for Web browsers named *Roadster*. In the words of Allegiant: "Based on Allegiant Technologies' award-winning *SuperCard* authoring tool, *Roadster* is the most flexible and powerful plug-in for delivering true interactive multimedia applications within popular Web browsers such as *Netscape Navigator* and Microsoft *Internet Explorer*" [URL E]. As this software develops, we can expect to see some very interactive *SuperCard* programs delivered using the WWW. During my test of the software, I saw many problems but, at the same time, outstanding capabilities (Figure 9.22).

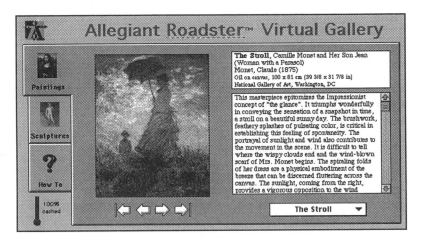

Figure 9.22. Screen capture from the Roadster Art Gallery project developed in *SuperCard* and played over the Web using *Roadster* plug-in.

## Macromedia *Director/Shockwave*

*Director* is a program well suited for multimedia interaction. In fact, it may be the program of choice for developers with large graphics budgets. *Director* already is a cross-platform product, with Mac and PC versions available.

WWW fever struck at Macromedia early, and a "plug-in" called *Shockwave* was developed. *Director*-developed materials played using *Shockwave* promise to play a very important role in WWW interactive materials. Taken from a Web site with frequently asked questions (faq) about *Shockwave*: "What is *Shockwave*? *Shockwave* for *Director*, by Macromedia, is a Plug-in for *Netscape Navigator 2.0* that enables the playback of multimedia on the World Wide Web. To obtain *Shockwave* for *Director*, visit Macromedia's Web site at http://www.macromedia.com/ and follow the links."

One of the notions of *ShockWave* is that it will stream information to the browser and begin "playing" once sufficient information is in hand. Figures 9.23, 9.24, and 9.25 are screen captures of a *Director* program being developed by Helen Brooks describing for chemical technicians the operation of a paper mill.

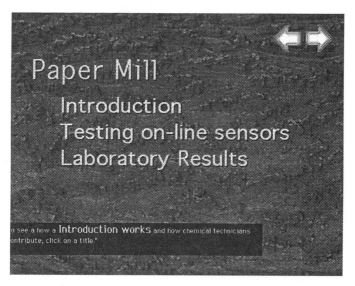

Figure 9.23. Macromedia *Director* "Stage."

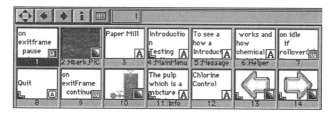

Figure 9.24. Macromedia *Director* "Cast."

## Applications (e.g., *Mathematica*)

*Mathematica*, first developed as a mathematician's tool, has evolved through several generations. At this time, efforts are being made to make interactive *Mathematica* notebooks available on the WWW. See p. 85.

## The Proposed *QuickTime* Revision

*QuickTime* is a Macintosh system extension developed by Apple that handles time-based data. When first released, *QuickTime* pioneered software-only movies for personal computers. Among the options emerging or promised on the horizon, the reincarnation of *HyperCard* as a product merged with *Quick-Time*, Apple's cross-platform multimedia format scheme [URL U], is very excit-

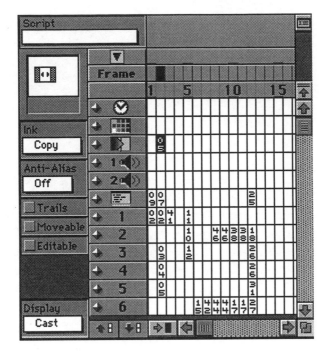

Figure 9.25.  Macromedia *Director* "Score."

ing.  This product was demonstrated at a developers conference in May1996, and received excellent comments from those present.  The delivery date was set for 1997, however, and many things can happen during that interval.


## JAVASCRIPT

The interactivity we seek is difficult to achieve with any media, especially on the WWW.  When the WWW first appeared, browsers were quite limited. Movies and animations then began to appear, and these brought screens to life — even if they did not provide interactivity.  The tools used to display molecular models, as described in Chapter 7, certainly have made an impact in chemistry education.  So have clickable maps, especially client-side maps.  Nevertheless, one wants more intelligence than this, and that intelligence should preferably be at the client side.

Recognizing this, there has been a very substantial effort to create tools.  A new computer language, Java, has been invented.  Even though this language really isn't here as of press time, most persons in the computer business expect it to take over *massive* chunks of the market.  There is much talk about personal computer operating systems becoming much more Internet friendly — of being optimized for Internet activities. There used to be talk like this when the U.S. military sought to develop a new language, Ada. My intuition is that Java will be more successful than Ada has been.

The Java environment is a portable, robust, high-performance, advanced language that offers the ease of use and functionality that object-oriented languages have always promised, but never quite attained. By providing a portable, dynamic, multithreading language, programmers can develop advanced applications across heterogeneous networks such as the Internet. At the same time, the class libraries impart the ease of use and functionality of more open platforms while providing a secure environment for distributed systems. These features in combination are sure to make Java the dominant technology of the Internet in the next decade.

With this information in mind, understanding the ways in which to both use and serve Java content becomes imperative. For most users, the primary use of Java will be either as stand-alone applications or as extensions and applets in a browser environment. ..."

Ritchey, 1996, p. 223

JavaScript, a "member of the Java language family," is an HTML scripting tool developed by Netscape. JavaScript is intended to provide greater intelligence for browsers. Teacher-authors can think up ways to develop this intelligence; authors of browser software will provide the tools for these teacher-authors as opposed to providing exactly what a teacher-author might decide she or he wants. Figure 9.26 shows a simple browser page for converting Celsius temperatures into Fahrenheit temperatures. Figure 9.27 shows the HTML file that is used to create the page.

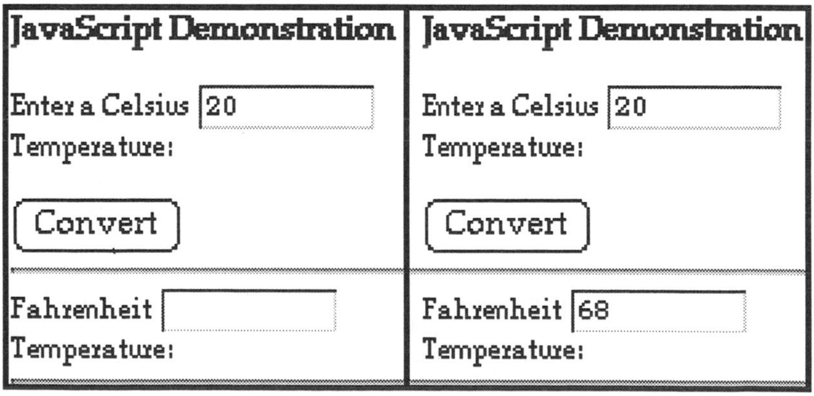

Figure 9.26. Browser page for converting Celsius to Fahrenheit temperatures. Left, before "Convert" button is clicked; right, after "Convert" button is clicked.

```
<!DOCTYPE HTML PUBLIC "-//IETF//DTD HTML 3.0//EN">
<HTML>
<HEAD>
<TITLE>Celsius to Fahrenheit Converter</TITLE>
<SCRIPT LANGUAGE="Javascript">
<!-- Hide javascript from old browsers.
function displayCF(){
document.CFCon.Celsius.blur();
document.CFCon.Fahrenheit.value = convertCF();
}
function convertCF() {
var celsiusT = document.CFCon.Celsius.value;
var fahrenheitT = (celsiusT * 9 / 5) + 32;
return fahrenheitT
}
function clearit(){
document.CFCon.Fahrenheit.value="";
}
// -->
</SCRIPT>
</HEAD>
<BODY>
<H3 ALIGN=LEFT>JavaScript Demonstration</H3>
<FORM  NAME="CFCon">
Enter a Celsius
<INPUT TYPE="text" NAME="Celsius" VALUE="37"
   SIZE="10" onFocus="clearit()"
   onBlur="displayCF()"><BR>
Temperature:<BR><BR>
<INPUT TYPE="button" Name="Convert"
VALUE="Convert" onClick="displayCF()">
<HR>
Fahrenheit <INPUT TYPE="text" NAME="Fahrenheit"
SIZE=10>
<BR>Temperature:
<HR>
</FORM>
</BODY>
</HTML>
```

Figure 9.27. HTML text file used to create the browser page shown in Figure 9.26.

It is not difficult to imagine creating some rather sophisticated questioning strategies for presentation on the client side as a result of JavaScript programming. For example, you might store banks of information for problems, enable random access to these banks, have learners respond by entering answers, and then judge the response. It is a matter of time until someone attempts to develop such materials using JavaScript.

Because Javascript won't permit massive file changes for security reasons, storing information at the client side is difficult. A cookie is a small entry of text information in a Netscape file. Cookies can be made persistent. Any intricate Javascript system for managing instruction on the client side is likely to make use of cookies.

## PROGRAMMING

As you can see through many examples in this book, creating successful interactive instructional materials very often requires programming. One way to make it happen is to learn how to do this yourself. Another is to hire student or professional programmers. Having others program for you is tricky; I don't know how many times I've been asked to untangle programs that have been created by student programmers, and left behind — poorly documented and difficult to maintain and update.

This approach is not without hope, however, even if the product is a good bit less than perfect. Remember, the *best* software developers commonly put out materials that are buggy — even when they have used numerous strategies to detect and correct bugs. If you farm out programming, be certain to spend a great deal of time browsing sites that are interactive and **bookmarking\*** URLs. Sometimes having examples to use is exactly what you'll need to make your programmers aware of what you want.

## JAVA

As noted, Java is a powerful language developed with the Internet in mind. One interesting example of how Java can be used appears at the MapQuest site where a Java applet allows users to "zero in" on any place in the United States (Figure 9.28).

Perhaps the most important feature of Java is that it compiles in the form of bytecode. Applications that create bytecode are platform specific, but the bytecode is generic. So, Java bytecode compiled on a Macintosh can be used directly by a Wintel computer using Wintel-specific Java implementation software. If this scheme really works out as planned, problems of portability may begin to disappear. Because the bytecode is not likely to be as efficient as machine-specific machine code, sacrifices in speed are expected. For nearly all of the things I want to accomplish as a teacher, platform independence is much more desirable than speed, especially in a world where computers run ever faster.

*Visual Cafe* by Symantec is a new application that provides a remarkable developing environment for the creation of applications in Java.

## CGIS

The Common Gateway Interface, or CGI, is one of the most useful tools in a Webmaster's kit. Whether you're the lone maintainer of a single home page or someone else's machine or the Webmaster of a huge domain, you'll find that CGI is essential for anything beyond presenting static text and graphics.

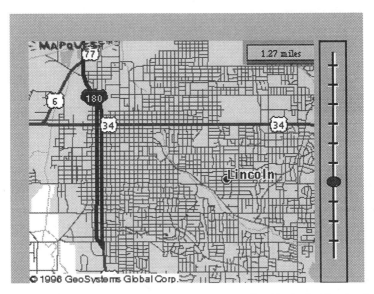

Figure 9.28. Screen capture from the MapQuest site [URL AD]. This site enables the display of maps at very high resolution. It makes use of a Java applet.

CGI is the magic behind Web-based interactive games, page counters, order-entry systems, on-line shopping carts, SQL database interfaces, animations, and **clickable images\***. In fact, you'll find that CGI, in one of its many forms, is what brings the World Wide Web to life."

Dwight and Erwin, 1996, p. 1

The large book on my shelf, *Using CGI* by Dwight and Erwin [1996], is thorough and extensive. In spite of this, it devotes about one-half of one page to using *HyperCard* for the task of handling CGIs. *HyperCard* is the principal method I use. This does not speak to inadequacies in the book, but rather to the extent of the problem. CGI applications represent programming. As nearly always is the case, when programming is involved there is more than one way to attack a problem.

My choice of *HyperCard* was a simple one; I know HyperTalk, the *HyperCard* programming language, very well. I could create useful Web applications as soon as I got the hang of "talking" back and forth with my server software. Using *WebStar* for this purpose makes it a simple matter. I took one sample program from the WWW, saw how the HyperTalk was written, tried it until I "got it right," and have been using *HyperCard* ever since. The program (Figure 9.29) that creates individualized chemistry quizzes upon request was developed in *HyperCard*.

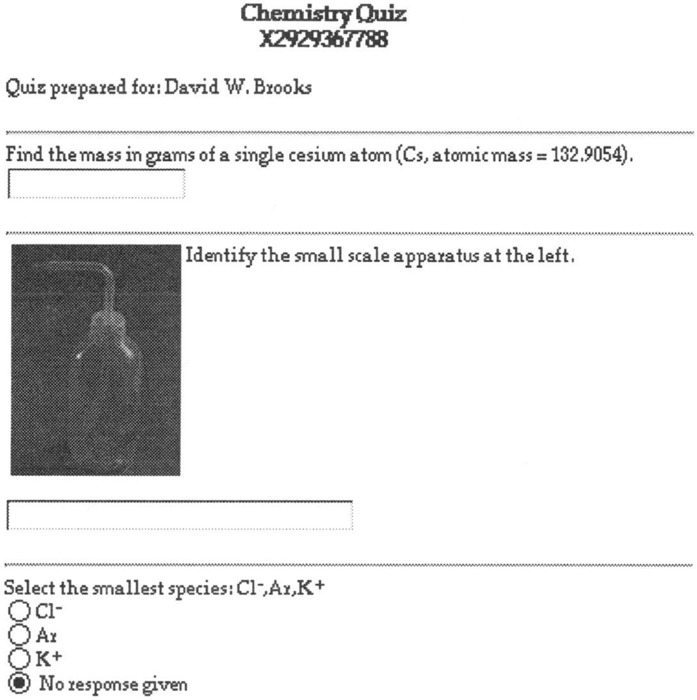

**Chemistry Quiz**
**X2929367788**

Quiz prepared for: David W. Brooks

Find the mass in grams of a single cesium atom ($Cs$, atomic mass = 132.9054).

[                    ]

Identify the small scale apparatus at the left.

[                              ]

Select the smallest species: $Cl^-$, $Ar$, $K^+$
○ $Cl^-$
○ $Ar$
○ $K^+$
◉ No response given

Figure 9.29.   Sample chemistry questions created using a *HyperCard* cgi at the author's Web site.

Writing CGIs *is* a big deal.   If you're a teacher with no programming skills, you'll need help.   The kind of help you need can be available on two levels.   One is to find a student who is very computer literate and knows some programming to search the WWW for CGI freeware.   You'll find plenty of software.   Have them adapt what they find for your task.   At the next level, you need a student still wiser in the ways of bits and bytes, one who can create CGI applications from scratch.   If you have no access to such students, then you'll need to find a professional programmer.

As time goes on, the process of creating CGIs will be made simpler and simpler.   The server software will be enhanced over and over again in attempts to facilitate using CGIs.   You'll see authoring tools that will do for the task of creating CGIs what currently available tools do for tagging files with HTML. Never expect this process to become very simple, however, unless you are willing to accept the programming constraints imposed by someone else.

How do my CGIs work?   Apple Macintosh has a scheme for exchanging information between programs at the system level called AppleEvents.   When the server software (*WebStar*) receives input from the client browser (like a form), it sends out an AppleEvent.   This message can be directed.   I've taken an alias of *HyperCard 2.3* and renamed it HC.cgi.   This alias behaves like *HyperCard*, but the ".cgi" MIME extension (Multipurpose Internet Mail Extension) makes it think it's something special, something that can serve as a common gateway interface application. I've modified the "Home" stack of *HyperCard*, the document that *HyperCard* always runs, so that it looks for AppleEvents. This Home document is always kept running at the top level of my server. When an AppleEvent aimed at the cgi comes to it, the Home stack gathers related information, parses the information, decides what program is called for, and goes to that program. I have separate *HyperCard* documents (stacks) for creating chemistry exams, gathering personal data for creating class rosters for each course, and so forth. The Home stack wakes up the targeted stack, sends information to it, and lets that stack handle the task of replying to *WebStar* with a document to return to the client. After this is all done, control is transferred back to the Home stack, a log with some information about the transaction is updated, and the system settles down to wait for it all to happen again.

In spite of the criticism that *HyperCard* is "slow," the transaction of either creating or evaluating a chemistry test usually takes less than 5 seconds from the time the client sends the form information until it receives a response. This is more than adequate to handle a course of, say, 100 students. It might be possible to tune it up to serve 1000 students, or to create much larger examinations.


## DATABASES; DATABASE CGIS

The emergence of Web-friendly interactive databases is occurring at press time. *FileMaker Pro* is a well-regarded relational database with a long, solid history. Recently *Tango*, an application that behaves like a cgi, has been developed to make *FileMaker Pro* databases function over the Web. The potential applications for such software in teaching are enormous.


## OTHER WAYS TO ENVISION CURRICULA

There are many ways to envision curricula and to frame the tasks provided for students. For example, in science there has been substantial interest in the informal educational opportunities offered by museums, and the National Science Foundation as well as other funding organizations have invested substantial sums toward these efforts.

In *Engines for Education*, Schank and Cleary [1995] suggest that "people have powerful natural mechanisms for learning that allow them to master an enormous volume and variety of material during their lifetimes." Their book suggests five ways of natural learning: simulation-based learning by doing; incidental learning; learning by reflection; case-based teaching; and learning by exploring.

If you're dissatisfied with conventional approaches to instruction and would like to take a look at other views, *Engines for Education* offers many interesting perspectives. For example, incidental learning makes use of finding some activity that is inherently pleasurable to undertake and coupling some learning to that activity. Since the thrust of *Engines for Education* is to point readers toward computer materials, readers of *Web-Teaching* are likely to find it especially interesting.

Figure 9.30. Screen capture from example program found in *Engines for Education* CD-ROM dealing with sickle-cell anemia. In the program, students role-play through the intermediacy of a computer program. They hear patients speak, take blood, perform lab tests, etc. The program makes it possible for them to become active learners rather than just readers of facts about this problem. With permission.

# CHAPTER 10

## PROMOTION OF SELF-REGULATED LEARNING

This chapter is about making students better at academic survival. Think about what you are proposing to undertake. You are now contemplating putting much of your learning material "on-line." In your current setting, you have some control. To some degree, you can make students attend class. (This varies from setting to setting, of course.) You can engage them in activities. Over the WWW, they have much more freedom. They may be logged onto a machine, but you won't be there to see what they're actually doing. My sense is that students who are poor at self-regulation easily can be "slaughtered" in WWW-based courses. You can't place your materials on the WWW if your candidate students are not self-regulating and hope for success, can you?

In November 1995, Christy Horn presented a seminar based on her doctoral research and subsequent extensions of that work. She described the results of studies of introductory biology classes (at a major Midwestern university) [Horn *et al.*, 1993; Horn, 1993, 1995]. The bottom line of her work is that the biggest fraction of lack of success can be attributed to students' *not trying!* Worse yet, this problem is not localized; it is widespread at "major" universities. Students who do not attend classes do not interact with the learning materials and, therefore, have very low success. Until her presentation, I had no idea about the extent of documentation available, nor the breadth of this troubling situation. This result is extremely disconcerting. After all, instructors can do only so much to improve their teaching before the lack of student involvement becomes a limiting factor.

There is substantial hope for improvement, however. As one of several responses to Horn's results, faculty have developed Web pages for student use. For example, one UNL biology instructor [Glider, 1996] has developed a Web page with the opportunity for submitting questions, tutorials, old quizzes with answers and discussion, and enrichment materials. Questions are entered using standard HTML form elements. His early sense is that the page has led to improved student learning.

Self-regulation concerns the entire range of factors that affect student performance. Intelligence is an extremely controversial construct describing factors about which teacher impact is limited at best. Self-regulation is something that is teachable and not irreversibly constrained by intelligence [Symons *et al.*, 1989]. Self-regulation accounts for the ability of persons of modest intelligence to become skilled masters of very complex tasks.

My interest in self-regulation previously had been piqued by Gregg Schraw: here is something a teacher can hope to impact in students' lives. To hear Schraw tell the tale, it may well be the most important thing a teacher can do for students; it may amount to empowering them to be lifelong learners. This kind of thinking pervades the community of educational psychologists studying these issues:

> A new vision of education is emerging. It is one in which children are provided procedural instruction throughout their academic careers, one in which strategy instruction is at the heart of education. This reflects the belief that a major goal of schooling is to teach people *how* to read, write, and solve problems.
>
> Symons *et al.*, 1989, p. 1

While there is reason to be very optimistic, there still is every reason to acknowledge that enhanced performance resulting from some training about self-regulation is unlikely to work miracles. Most of what *Web-Teaching* deals with concerns teaching and learning beyond grade 7, with an emphasis on advanced high school, college, graduate education, and industrial training. When good jobs are involved, it is an easy matter to see how to improve self-regulation. Indeed, good suggestions to improve one's performance are likely to be welcomed and embraced quickly. For most students in school, however, those who are poor self-regulators are unlikely to be quickly changed in spite of the hope that enhancements can be taught to nearly all learners.

## SELF-REGULATION

Self-regulation is a relatively new construct in research on learning. Self-regulated learners attempt to adjust the characteristics of their behavior, motivation, and cognition to fit the task at hand. Perhaps most important, control and goal setting come from within the student; they are not externally imposed.

> Self-regulated learning involves the active, goal-directed, self-control of behavior, motivation and cognition for academic tasks by an individual student.
>
> Pintrich, 1995, p. 5

Interest in enhancing student self-regulation relates to compensatory effects. Given two persons with different skills, one with very high knowledge but low self-regulation, and the other with average knowledge but good self-regulation, the second person is more likely to be successful at a task in the given knowledge area than is the first. Self-regulated learners actively control the learning environment. They schedule appropriate amounts of time. They find physical environments appropriate for their effective study. They plan having materials ready. They plan human resources as needed, e.g., peer helpers and tutors. Self-regulated learners work to control their motivation. They find ways to deal with anxiety. They opt for study time instead of electronic games time. Finally, self-regulated learners choose cognitive strategies that have higher payouts. They seek to understand ideas and material rather than just memorize and recall.

> *Motivation* is the process whereby goal-directed activity is instigated and sustained.
>
> Pintrich and Schunk, 1996, p. 4

Of course, we'd all like students to be self-regulated learners. Indeed, we ourselves strive to be self-regulated. If you're reading this book, you're almost certainly self-regulated. This book might find its way to being a text in a few graduate courses, but more likely it will be read by teachers seeking to improve their teaching. So, if you're reading this page, you're self-regulating to some serious degree. How do we teach our students to be self-regulating?

> Self-regulated learning is a way of approaching academic tasks that students learn through experience and self-reflection. It is not a characteristic that is genetically based or formed early in life so that students are "stuck" with it for the rest of their lives."
>
> Pintrich, 1995, pp. 4–5

## PRINCIPLES FOR ENCOURAGING SELF-REGULATION

Self-regulation is a new-enough construct that there still is a lack of study of how to make it work for more students more often. In fact, there still is dispute among experts as to how generalizable self-regulation strategies are, particularly as they pertain to understanding one's own cognition [Borkowski *et al.*, in press].

It shouldn't surprise anyone that tests of strategies for teaching this material using the WWW are not available. In fact, there are two extremes of WWW instruction. At one end, you'll be using a small portion of course supplementary material on the WWW; at the other, nearly the entire course will be Web-delivered. Obviously the ways in which you, the teacher, might go about working to enhance self-regulating skills in students will be a function of the situation in which you operate.

## Focus on Content Mastery, Not Just Task Mastery

The tone of Horn's dissertation is much less disquieting than was her seminar. In her dissertation, she attempted to determine factors that contributed to student success in college biology. There still are many more studies about these factors in the K–12 domain of schooling than for college. She describes mastery goal orientation as "a concern with increasing competence, [that] leads students to view difficult tasks as challenges and to confront difficulties by more completely analyzing tasks, altering strategies, and increasing their efforts." Horn reached the following conclusion:

> Rather than assessing what was needed to complete the task assigned to them, mastery oriented individuals apparently approached the task of learning biology as a knowledge construction task which led to increased performance on the classroom performance tasks, as well as the knowledge construction tasks.
>
> Horn, 1993, pp. 52–53

It seems clear that teachers might want to focus on content mastery rather than task mastery. Perhaps one way to do this is to explicitly tie assignments to content mastery, and to point out the relationships explicitly.

## Increase Student Awareness of Their Own Self-Regulation

Self-monitoring is the basis for awareness of one's self-regulation. In some ways it is akin to an architect's plans for a house versus the "as builts" — what actually was done. It is hard to get self-monitoring to happen, especially to get students to disembed actions or processes from complex contexts, and to relate them to outcomes.

Journaling is one of the most common strategies used by teachers. Journaling has been encouraged at the University of Nebraska–Lincoln for over 20 years. It would be a bad idea for you to have students keep journals on-line, or to have them all shared over the WWW. However, you might be able to get some volunteer journals, provide them as examples, and encourage those volunteers to create accompanying analyses.

Another approach you might take is to create sets of materials and offer students different ways of approaching learning those materials. Develop systematic assessments, and try to tie the performance to the approach. For example, one week you might have students log on to the Web daily for 30 minutes, and compare their results with logging on for one 2 to 3 hour session during the next week. When did they achieve better learning? (You could incorporate the same strategy for testing the impact of duration of study into a weblet on a CD-ROM.)

You might have students begin some material by going to old exams, as opposed to reading the material first. Do they do better when practice exams precede or follow the exposure to the content?

Having a narrow focus for self-monitoring gives better results than having a broad focus [Shapiro, 1984]. This is a good role for the teacher — to dissect tasks, and focus on their parts. When all is said and done, you probably get to give one grade for the student, and at most you write several paragraphs. There are probably scores of tasks that go into making these letter grades and paragraphs what they are. As a teacher, focus on those that are most productive, cause the most difficulty, or are least appreciated by your students, *but focus*.

One thing that might be important is to have students monitor procrastination. This might uncover patterns useful for improving performance. For example, procrastination when logging onto the WWW might reveal times when machine response is slow, and lead to the formal, conscious decision to plan logging on during times when responses are faster.

That probably sounds trivial to you. After all, if you're on this page, you're probably an effective self-regulating learner yourself, and you can't believe that students might not notice this phenomenon immediately and adjust their schedules accordingly. Wrong! The phenomenon can go totally unnoticed.

One of the hardest things to do with college students is to get them to undertake self-monitoring. In the absence of some serious external intervention, students can just muddle along. In fact, even when students can be shown that monitoring improves knowledge of performance, there still can be a problem. Schraw [1994] noted substantial discrepancies between actual performance and knowledge of what works best. (It's like smoking; very few smokers still believe that smoking is good for them, or even that it is without effect.)

## Engender Positive, Realistic Views of Student Self-Efficacy

Self-regulated learning is generally viewed as a fusion of *skill* and *will*.

Garcia, 1995, p. 29

Self-efficacy beliefs are incredibly important. These are task and context specific, and cannot necessarily be generalized from self-esteem or self-worth. Horn's seminar presented results in this area that were downright scary. In spite of all sorts of evidence that they were doing poorly in a class for which they had not learned the material, many students believed that things would work out well for them in the end.

Often, when a student believes she has no chance of learning materials because she is not smart enough or hasn't had the right opportunities, then a situation opposite that mentioned above may set in. Sometimes students engage in a self-handicapping strategy. In anticipation of a poor result, they perform less.

Then, when the bad result arrives, they can always say they could have done it, but chose not to do it.

On the other hand, sometimes having low expectations in an area deemed necessary pays off. Some students concerned about poor performance make use of this "defensive pessimism" [Norem and Cantor, 1986]. They work very hard to overcome poor performance — studying, putting forth a strong effort. In this way, if they perform poorly they are not so disappointed by the outcome. On the other hand, they have used this to muster and apply personal learning resources in ways likely to avoid the poor performance. The point is that high levels of learning are not always driven by high self-efficacy and high competence.

A good result from taking a practice test would be to provide the feedback, "If you perform this way on the course exam, you'll get a C+." That's the kind of feedback you can build into practice tests at your Web site.

The Keller Plan strategy [Keller and Sherman, 1974], in which students were required to reach a certain level before they could go on, dealt with this problem. Keller's strategies worked very well for courses, but were abandoned for many reasons. Two of the reasons involved the higher demand on teachers and the higher demand on students engendered when a minimum learning standard is adopted. In a sense, it required that all of our students be above average.

## Model Self-Regulated Learning

Without a doubt, my own modeling of self-regulation involves talking out loud as I work through problems. I'm best when I get stuck and have to concentrate and "think hard." Some students find this very frustrating, especially when I go into some hypothesis testing, follow some student input with a long series of questions that leads to some nonsense, and then wait for them to say, "hey, that's nonsense." Many times I let nonsense stand. If half a period goes by before someone finally gets to say, "hey, that's nonsense," student frustration levels can be very high. This is especially true for students who see me as an authority figure and source of knowledge. You just can't do this sort of thing on the WWW! Unless you have some sort of active cooperative learning community in place and functioning critically, "nonsense" needs to be corrected early.

If you can anticipate confusion and/or misconceptions, then you can create a trail of clicks that lead to a Web-based dead end, that is, a path that leads to a conclusion that flies in the face of reality.

## Provide Practice for Self-Regulated Learning Strategies

One thing that makes a great deal of sense is to have students work with "infinite" exam banks of the type that are readily generated for the WWW. Students can see numerous questions, and they can see the related worked-out examples. The support for using worked-out examples is very strong [Pressley and McCormick, 1995].

## Make Your WWW Tasks Opportunities for Student Self-Regulation

The most strongly advocated approach to including opportunities for student self-regulation is to give students choices. Experience also suggests that challenging tasks stimulate self-regulation better than do routine or boring tasks. Setting a mastery orientation for the material is good. To whatever degree possible, this can be achieved by tying the learning to future goals in some meaningful way. I do think this can be overdone, and that teachers often not only seek to tie everything to a student's future, but also shy away from content, particularly abstract content, that may not seem directly relatable.

My own view of this centers around a concept called just-in-time learning. In this notion, expert systems (often called electronic performance support systems) are developed to teach persons (workers) what they need to know about something just at the moment they need to know it [URL AK]. That may work for knowing which federal regulations apply in determining benefits for a Medicaid recipient. I don't expect to see just-in-time calculus anytime soon, and I *do* think knowing calculus has lots of value for all learned persons, not just scientists and engineers.

## EXPLICIT TRAINING

Providing explicit training about strategies, particularly to college students, may be a valuable investment of time. My work supervising student teachers brings me to high school classrooms in Nebraska on a regular basis. High schools are not always breeding grounds for effective self-regulation. There often is setting of low levels of expected performance, alternatives for those who do not perform successfully, and a pervasive notion that all of the work be accomplished in the classroom — with little or no outside-of-class effort required.

For these reasons, college teachers, especially those in large introductory courses, should consider explicit instruction about self-regulation. For example, it may be well worth your time to point out the need for finding a quiet place to study and planning adequate time for study while the student is fresh enough for the study to be effective. Students need to know that daydreaming time must be subtracted from total time to get an idea of how much effort has been expended. In some home environments, a parent externally imposes restrictions about study time and place. When these are removed as when attending a residential college, the student simply is not aware of their absence.

Another important feature is control of attention. Study is not like a video game where you must attentively track some screen icon or note some event to avoid disaster. Students must self-monitor their attention and, further, do things to control that attention.

Formal instruction about self-regulation is appropriate. It can work for all of us. I find myself losing entire days when three students come in to see me. If I schedule them one after another, I only gab too much with the last one. Suggestions about controlling motivation are useful. I sometimes feel that having a formal reading of *The Little Engine That Could* is a valuable college exercise [e.g., as retold by Piper, 1984, 1930]. You also might consider explicit strategies for students related to writing class notes. In a WWW-based course, having formal activities in which the students consolidate and organize what they have learned may be very necessary.

## DISCIPLINE-SPECIFIC SELF-REGULATION

### Implicit Conventions

Every profession has rules that are implicit. Sometimes we professionals are so far from our roots that we take these rules for granted. For example, in chemistry, when a balanced chemical equation does not have a numerical coefficient written in front of each formula, then those numbers are assumed to be ones (unity).

A very important task of the instructor is to try to make explicit as much of the "implicit stuff" as possible. A very good way to do this in a live, face-to-face classroom is to have the instructor tackle a problem that is ill-defined. When doing the problem, the instructor should try to "talk out loud," step by step, as she works the problem. Although many of my graduate chemistry instructors were good at this strategy, none was better than Gilbert Stork, a world-renowned synthetic organic chemist. In Stork's teaching, there was one after another verbalized rhetorical question followed by his discussion of the answer. We students listened as he spoke out loud to himself. It was not at all interactive, but it was wonderful. I suspect it would have driven nearly all of the "non-organic" chemistry graduate students insane. For this strategy to work, the problem can't be too simple or routine. At the same time, it can't be too complex. In mathematics or physics, for example, doing a routine end-of-chapter problem is likely to be so automatic for the instructor that the implicit steps are chunked and handled so quickly that they are not revealed during a discussion of the problem.

At this moment in my own thinking, I remain unsure about how to accomplish this instruction over the WWW. I think I would rely on the strategy of worked-out problems, perhaps with inclusion of some blind alleys not usually included with such solutions.

## Overarching Notions and Ways of Thinking

There are three ways to view chemistry. There is a macroscopic view — what the eye normally sees. There is a submicroscopic view — the atomic and molecular level models that chemists invoke to explain the macroscopic phenomena. Finally, there is a symbolic view — a way of using elemental symbols and chemical formulas and other symbol systems to represent chemical changes [Greenbowe, 1983; Herron, 1996]. It probably is very worthy for chemistry teachers to make explicit these ways of thinking. Essentially every profession has its models and icons and symbols and ways of viewing the world. Making these explicit to novice learners is a key task in instruction.

## Experts versus Novices

Much research is being expended to compare the ways experts and novices tackle problems in disciplines. One of the worthy missions teachers can undertake is not only to try to make explicit the ways in which they undertake problems, but also to try to indicate problems with the ways novices often undertake the same problems. For example, while experts in physics are making sketches about a problem, novices are likely to be plugging available numbers into some formula. Experts try to get down to what's what early in the game.

## EXAMS

Using the WWW, there may be a temptation to make exams easier than you would otherwise. In particular, there may be a trap related to rewarding memorization and rote. This is a serious potential pitfall, one that works against engendering effective self-regulation in your students. Remember, when all else fails, have learners write essays that are e-mailed to you. If there is a standard course word processor (*Word*, *ClarisWorks*), then you can have elaborate documents with embedded figures and spreadsheets, attached to their e-mail. A strategy I've used with great success is called repeatable testing [Moore *et al.*, 1977]. Students are given the option of repeating every test and earning a score equal to the average of their two tests. As I get older, I think more and more that the best results come from demanding minimum standards for parts of a course, and sticking to those standards come hell or high water.

## VIDEOCONFERENCING

I expect to use much of my WWW-based videoconferencing to work with individual students and small groups of students in the areas of self-regulation. I see this electronic face-to-face opportunity, coupled with the electronic whiteboards, as the best way for me to try to capture for the WWW what I now have in person.

# CHAPTER 11

## CREATING AND MANAGING WEB SITES

If you can access the WWW, then you also may have the ability to create a Web site at your computer. This chapter deals with issues related to managing a Web site. If you are a high school or college teacher, then your school probably already has one or several Web sites. My server is hard-wired to my university's network; there is no modem. Most University of Nebraska–Lincoln (UNL) rooms are outfitted with one or several outlets having two computer ports and one phone port. These are centrally controlled; one calls to have a particular port activated. Once a port is live, a department or some other agency is billed monthly for that port.

One of the ports in my room is more or less dedicated to a server, a Power Macintosh 6150 with installed *WebStar* software (see Figure 2.4). The most difficult part of setting up a server involved waiting for the arrival of the computer. The server was the first Mac 6150 purchased at my school.

When a computer or board has ethernet, a unique number is assigned to that device. These numbers are doled out by manufacturers. Software is available to poll the computer to ascertain its ethernet number or address. *Get My Address* or *Apple LAN Utility* works in the Macintosh world.

Your school or organization also has a scarce commodity to dole out, namely, **IP addresses\*** (Internet Protocol addresses). These are sets of four 8-bit numbers. At the University of Nebraska, we have all of the numbers that start with 129.93. The particular server I've mentioned was assigned the address 129.93.84.115 by UNL. That computer has the ethernet identification 08:00:07:6F:5E:32 assigned either by Apple Computing or one of its suppliers.

The server is nearly always on. Whenever it is turned on, the UNL network and the server exchange information with one another. The computer tells UNL its number, and the UNL system assigns it an address.

If you know the four numbered parts of a server's address, you know much of what you need to know about sending requests to it. The numbers, however, nearly always lack the elegance and/or memorability found in a name. (The date of birth of a relative of mine is 01/23/45. Few numbers permit such easy recall.) As a result, IP addresses are paired with **domain names\***. All or nearly all U.S. universities have addresses ending in edu. As it turns out, one of my faculty colleagues was at the National Science Foundation at the time that NSF-net expanded. So, the numbers at UNL translate to include unl.edu. The unl string would fit many schools; we were lucky to get it! Since mine was to be a Web server, and since I work at the Center for Curriculum and Instruction, I negotiated with the person at my school who assigns names for the following domain name:

**www.cci.unl.edu**

So, on the WWW 129.93.84.115 and www.cci.unl.edu mean the same thing. The number sequence gives less trouble than the letter sequence even though the numbers are very difficult to remember. You may wonder why so much time has been spent on this topic. Having a "neat" domain address might help your teaching, but it's not required. Once you have a valid address, hardware, a connection to the Internet, and server software, *you're ready to serve.*

Whenever I teach Web-teaching at some site other than Nebraska, I contact StarNine by e-mail to obtain a temporary password for *WebStar*. Once inside the teaching laboratory at the "remote" site, I select a computer to be the temporary teaching server and use *Get My Address* software to obtain that computer's IP address. I then download a trial copy of *WebStar*, install the software on that machine, and use the number obtained from the *Get My Address* software as the address. When requested during installation, I use the temporary password supplied by StarNine. When I leave the site a few days later, I trash the software and all of the teaching files that are loaded into that folder. The computer is restored to being just another lab computer. It *is* that simple!

An alias of the *WebStar* software is located in the "Start Up" folder of my UNL server. That way, when a Midwest power storm causes a momentary power outage that cuts off the current to my computer, the server usually restarts itself once the power comes back on. Also, when I travel, I ask a student to log on to the server daily and, if something is not right, to come into the office and reset the computer.

If you are using a modem, you probably won't want to become a server site. It will be very difficult to keep your site up and running all the time.


## HARDWARE

Nearly any Macintosh computer can be a server. Used computer systems that have a street value under $1000 work well. I have colleagues using old hardware to serve small numbers of students working at locations in western Nebraska. For example, a Mac IIci or IIcx equipped with an inexpensive ethernet board will satisfy most small server needs very well.

The speed with which information moves over the network and not some internal limit determines how fast most documents can be served from my server. *HyperCard*-based software processes complex server requests for tests and enrollments. The requests are processed in 2–4 seconds. That time could be reduced significantly if needed. However, turnaround time is not a problem. Characteristic sounds (earcons) are emitted from the server when *HyperCard* requests are processed, and these give everyone in my office a good feel for what is going on in terms of what is being transacted and how long it is taking. The Mac 6150 is more than adequate for current needs. It crunches complex *Hyper-Card* programs very quickly. Once I was running a workshop from a good site at the University of Massachusetts making connections back to Nebraska. Files are served in a few seconds, but busy signals were sent when all 18 student stations called for the files within the same few moments. By immediately repeating their requests, the UNL server never gave a busy two times in a row to the same station in Massachusetts.

Without having any experience in the Wintel world, I can't be sure this is true, but there is no apparent reason why a Wintel machine would not give similar performance for the same reasons when running server software.

Persons with servers receiving many "hits" per day usually choose more powerful hardware. Sun Microsystems provides many such systems, particularly in a family known as *Sparc* stations [URL Y]. Servers often are **UNIX**\*-based. Most faculty at UNL use a UNL server, and do not have "private" servers on our network.

If I'm ever involved in a situation where I need to serve very large numbers of clients, then I'm going to first try to deal with the network speed. Line speed usually is the weak link.

> Despite the increasing number of Web (i.e., HTTP) servers in use each day, little is definitively known about their performance characteristics. We present a simple, high-level, open queuing network model from which we derive several general performance results for Web servers on the Internet. Multiple-server systems are also analyzed. A theoretical upper bound on the serving capacity of Web servers is defined. As Web servers approach this boundary response times increase suddenly toward infinity, disabling the server; but limiting the server's simultaneous connections prevents this problem.
>
> URL S

## SOFTWARE

*MacHTTP* was developed by Chuck Shotton. He went from providing shareware to selling through a company, StarNine, under the name *WebStar*. StarNine has been bought by Quarterdeck. In April 1996, a survey of Web sites conducted by the Graphics, Visualization, and Usability Center at the Georgia

Institute of Technology showed about 25% of sites surveyed using *Webstar* software [URL C]. *NetSite* was described as a Netscape product, but a call to Netscape indicated different product names. Netscape also sells server software under the name *SuiteSpot*.

*WebStar* is extremely easy to use. After a simple installation, one merely double-clicks the software's icon. All files at the level of the *WebStar* software, or in folders lower in the hierarchy, can be served. This includes html, GIF and jpg , hqx, mov, and other files. From beginning the installation process to actually running your server takes less than 10 minutes, and possibly less than 5 minutes.

Suppose you create a file named default.html and place it in the folder at the level of the *WebStar* program on a machine named 129.93.84.115. The default.html looks like Figure 11.1.

```
<HTML>
<HEAD>
<TITLE>WWW.CCI.UNL   A Description.</TITLE
<BODY BGCOLOR=#FFFF95>
<H2 ALIGN=CENTER><A NAME="Top"><IMG SRC="H
</A></H2>
This server offers resources related to th
HREF="http://www.cci.unl.edu/CVs/David_W..
his students and research collaborators a
Instruction, University of Nebraska-Linco

Extensive construction has been and contir
Please forgive errors and inconsistencies
HREF="mailto:dbrooks@unlinfo.unl.edu">Plec
<HR>
<H3>Resources</H3>

<B>Courses.</B> Courses includes course mc
David Brooks -- syllabi, lesson plans, ass
<P><UL><LI>

 <A HREF="http://www.cci.unl.edu/Courses/(
descriptions</A>.<BR><BR>
```

Figure 11.1. Sample of tagged file used as the "top" file at the service site 129.93.84.115.

Going to some browser on the WWW and entering:
**http://129.93.84.115**

will bring up a screen that looks something like Figure 11.2.

Figure 11.2. Partial screen capture of site reached. This outcome is the result of the browser software accessing "default.html" and one image file from the server at 129.93.84.115.

If you are using a server centralized at some university or school, then you'll frequently be downloading files, changing files, and so forth. You probably should get some help early on to learn to do this on your own. You are likely to need permissions and passwords, and these may not be readily forthcoming. I neither advocate nor discourage setting up a personal server. My message is that setting up and running your own device is no big deal. Complexity of operation is not the issue. It's more a matter of costs, maintenance, and security. I'm fully responsible for my server — all aspects. Sometimes it's a much easier way of life to have someone else running your server for you.

As already noted, I have my server set so that, when it goes down, it tries to start up again. At this moment, my "CGIs" are not in an automatic mode. When these go down, I need to go to the machine and restart them by hand.

## SITE ORGANIZATION

The issue of site organization is intertwined with the issue of security. Security is discussed in Chapter 13. When you organize a site, you are really talking about how folders and files are arranged. Figure 11.3 shows how the files are arranged on my site.

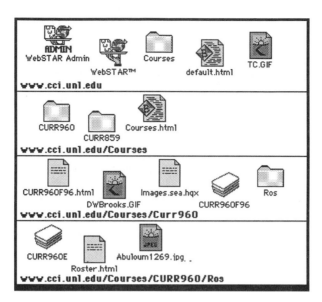

Figure 11.3. Schematic of the layout of the server in the author's office. See text for explanation.

Note that all of the visuals related to a file are kept in a single folder named with the same character string as the file. We serve substantial amounts of software. It has proven wise to keep copies of the most current copies of the software with the served HTML files.

When one uses the URL "http://www.cci.unl.edu", the file that is served is named default.html. So, at this site, the "default.html" file is very specific. It tells users about the site. All other files of interest are in folders at this level. For example, there is a folder named "Courses." At one time I used the name "default.html" for every folder file. This made typing of URLs easier for my users, but it was much too confusing for me. Now, after the main level of the site, a file with the same name as the folder followed by the MIME extension ".html" is in every folder. For a list of courses, the URL is "http://www.cci.unl.edu/Courses/Courses.html".

The file "Courses.html" points to the various courses for which information is available. One of the courses is Curriculum and Instruction 960, a course dealing with the subject matter of this book. So, to find out about that course, the URL is "http://www.cci.unl.edu/Courses/CURR960/CURR960F96.html". This file is a syllabus. The file itself is generated from a *HyperCard* stack that allows me to create syllabi in a format I find useful. (This *HyperCard* stack, named *Syllabus*, is available as freeware from the site.) Both the original and the appropriately packaged derivatives of any materials I serve out to students for the course are at this level. In this case, for example, a package of programs about images is served. These are bundled into a folder, compacted and converted into BinHex 4.0 format using *CompactPro*, a very useful utility.

There is still another level at the site with my class roster and the program that generates that roster. This also is a *HyperCard* stack that is used together with a special Home stack to serve as a sort of "cgi." Students enter roster information from any site on the WWW.

Whenever a situation arises where there are many image files to serve, I often put all of them in a folder with a name ending in GIFs (e.g., Abstract_GIFs). This happens most often when there are instruction manuals about using software. Some of these sets of instructions have nearly 100 image files.

# CHAPTER 12

# WEBLETS, CD-ROMS

This chapter speaks to ways of dealing with Web traffic and controlling student access. When students access your materials from home or off-campus, they are at the mercy of Web traffic. Web traffic sometimes can become a problem on campus during busy periods. Also, on the WWW, students can surf wherever they please. In schools and on campuses, especially in precollege settings, you may prefer to control student access to the WWW. There are two reasons to impose control. In both precollege and college classrooms, you can put *all* of the materials of interest to you on a local server, hard drive, optical drive, or CD-ROM. The resulting **weblet\*** is self-contained, and therefore can run as fast as your *local* network or drives permit. When you click a link, you are connected to another file on your network and not somewhere out on the Web. Also, the student cannot get into objectionable material on school premises starting out from your materials. This is a big issue with many parents, and therefore is of real importance in precollege settings. Remember, however, that what you are doing in creating a weblet is removing the most powerful feature of the WWW, namely, world wide connectivity.

A CD-ROM is a read-only storage medium with a large capacity. Today ROMs can hold 640 megabytes. Soon this capacity is expected to increase by a factor of ten or more; also, rewritable CDs are emerging. CD-ROMs can be constructed so that the data on them are accessible to both principal desktop computing worlds, the PC *and* the Macintosh.

It's getting so that buying a computer *without* a built-in CD-ROM drive is becoming more and more difficult. Software manufacturers have learned that ROMs afford a low-cost means for distributing software. There are fewer defects; more information of a peripheral nature can be provided at low cost; electronic manuals become possible, with printing costs transferred to the end user; and nearly all production costs go down. Teachers might well begin thinking about providing course materials for students on CD-ROMs. Making CD-ROMs one at a time has become rather easy and inexpensive.

There are alternatives that you might want to consider. For example, you could offer course materials on a "removable" drive medium instead of the permanent CD-ROM medium. You can have a locked source with one or several Syquest or Iomega Zip or Jaz drives, or the like, set up in a resource center. Students can bring blank disks to these sites, and copy massive amounts of information. This may be a better solution for a group of 50 students than the CD-ROM. It favors the teacher who is not fully prepared with all planned materials at the beginning of a course. Students must be able to access the chosen medium, and this presents a dissemination issue quite different from CD-ROMs. Your copying lab, then, might need to have a half-dozen or more drives to handle most student needs.

For nearly all of the courses I teach, I don't employ any of these approaches. I put nearly all of my material up on the WWW, and let the students get it down in whatever ways suit them best. If I were teaching our large, multisection technology course for undergraduates, I'm fairly sure I would go to weblets. Since students in that course are not required to have PCs, and since the course is required of all undergraduates, I think I'd make my weblets local.

## OBTAINING WEB MATERIALS

The law about using Web materials created by others is evolving. Publishing on the WWW seems to put everything up for grabs — including those materials you've created at great personal expense. Creating weblets preserves your authoring rights in conventionally protected formats.

What about Web materials created by others that you want your students to access? Clearly, using the WWW to accomplish this is OK. Capturing copies of those materials and incorporating them into your weblet is much less clear. My suggestion is to ask permission before you copy. If the material is copyrighted, ask the copyright owner. If not, ask the Webmaster of the site.

*WebWhacker* and *Web Grabber* are programs that permit users to go to a site and copy much that is there. These are remarkable software packages not only in terms of what they accomplish but also in terms of the acceptance of that process. After all, would you permit strangers to come into your offices at all hours to make xerographic copies of your paper files? If you are creating a weblet, you'll need to decide how much "foreign" information you want to include, and then decide how you are going to go about obtaining that information with appropriate permissions.

## MAKING WEBLETS; CD-ROMS

To make weblets you need something like a removable hard drive (e.g., optical, Zip, Jaz, Syquest) or a ROM maker. Making ROMs has become much easier over the last 3 or 4 years.

Old CD-ROM drives limited throughput to something in the neighborhood of 125 kilobytes per second. In the world of video information, this rate is quite slow. At this writing, the marketplace is flooded with faster drives, and speeds over ten times faster than early ROMs are available.

*Toast Pro* software makes formatting of the ROM straightforward. Many companies, such as APS, sell hardware to make single ROMs [URL AM; Figure 12.1].

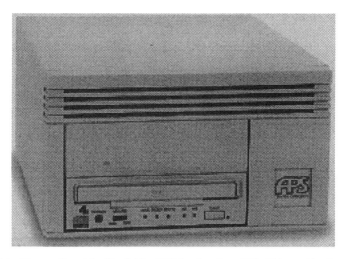

Figure 12.1. Picture of combined hard drive/ROM maker from APS. This combined system costs less than did either of its components just a few years ago when the author invested as much in a smaller hard drive as this entire unit costs today.

If you plan on making many disks, you'll need to work with a disk manufacturer. We've had a great deal of luck with Disc Manufacturing, Inc. "Disc Manufacturing, Inc., (DMI) is the leading independent Compact Disc mastering and manufacturing facility in the United States. DMI manufactures the entire spectrum of CD-ROM and CD-Audio formats at two sites in the U.S." [URL Z]. Figure 12.2 shows a CD-ROM manufactured by DMI.

Suppose you have a class of 50 students. Pressing 50 copies of a ROM, at the time of this printing, would cost less than $700. This cost has been decreasing steadily. Some pressing houses specialize in short runs, and can do a bit better. (The smallest run we've ever done is 500 ROMs.) If the student pays $15 for a ROM, the pressing cost is recovered. Many teachers ask students to pay much more than $15 for photocopied materials.

Copyrights must be handled legally. Not only is this a difficult issue, but it seems to become cloudier over time.

Getting the material ready to make the ROM can be extremely expensive and time consuming. The more material you have, the more costly the process can be. You need to keep this in mind — who pays for the time? If what you want to do is get 300 pages of material into your students' hands, ROMs start

Figure 12.2. CD-ROM developed under one of the author's projects. CD-ROMs are manufactured by a stamping process from a master. This project distributes 80 Mbytes of programs and information to high school chemistry teachers.

becoming attractive. As soon as you break into media such as movies, animations, and sounds, then ROMs become very, very attractive.

Students may want and sometimes need print copies. When the instructor provides a CD-ROM, the task and costs of creating the print copy are transferred to the student. Sometimes this is reasonable. My own direct experience with this, now 15 years old, is that students like print regardless of the cost. In 1980, all students were not happy about receiving microfiche copies of old exams. At the same time, they both used the microfiche *and* made print copies as needed and desired. At the time, printing from a microfiche was twice as expensive as ordinary paper copying. Most students were happy to have access to so much old exam material, however. As more and more colleges require that students obtain personal computing devices, you can expect to see increased use of CD-ROMs.

ROMs afford a physical object in possession and, therefore, a comforting mechanism for dealing with copyright issues. Physical objects — like books and magazines — are more in tune with our publishing past. Because ROMs can be used off-line, they afford a solution to the access/bandwidth problem often encountered by teachers using the WWW. Most ROM formats are read-only; read–write ROMs are not yet readily available, nor are erasable ROMs. There is a sense of archival documentation in the use of a ROM — being able to prove what was provided to users.

When using a ROM, use file references instead of http: calls. An appropriate HTML file is shown in Figure 12.3.

```
<HTML>
<HEAD>
<TITLE>TestXX</TITLE>
Show <A
HREF="file:///Macintosh%20HD/BalloonHelp.mov">
movie</A>.
</HEAD>
<BODY>
</BODY>
</HTML>
```

Figure 12.3. HTML file indicating ways to reference files for browser such as movies or sounds.

# CHAPTER 13

---

# SECURITY ISSUES; INTRANETS; COURSES FOR CREDIT

This chapter concerns security, copyright issues, and protecting faculty work. The WWW is published *everywhere*. Maybe that's not what you want.

> In the heterogeneous, hacker-happy world of the Internet, network managers can never be entirely sure of the safety of their networks. ...
> In a survey last year of more than 300 IS professionals and their network sites, the Computer Security Institute of San Francisco found that about 20 percent of organizations with an Internet connection admitted to suffering a "security incident."
>
> Streeter, 1996a, p. 33

If you have students taking Web-based exams, how will you handle sec rity?

## INTRANETS

An intranet uses the very same software as is used on the WWW. It gives all of your students, faculty, employees, and customers the same flexibility that WWW users have in terms of platforms and software. With an intranet, you control who has access to what. Needless to say, competition to provide material and services for developing intranets is very keen. The following text appears at the Netscape Web site:

> The Full Service Intranet is Netscape's vision of how companies can use standard Internet technologies to deploy a rich, full-function,

ubiquitous environment for information sharing, communication, and applications, built on top of open networking technologies and on an open network-based application platform.

The Full Service Intranet is a concept that Forrester Research first explored in a report of the same title dated March 1, 1996. Simply put, a Full Service Intranet is a TCP/IP network inside a company that links the company's people and information in a way that makes people more productive, information more accessible, and navigation through all the resources and applications of the company's computing environment more seamless than ever before.

The Full Service Intranet takes advantage of the family of open standards and protocols that have emerged from the Internet. These open standards make possible applications and services like e-mail, groupware, security, directory, information sharing, database access, and management that are as powerful, and in many cases more powerful, than traditional proprietary systems ... . Because the Full Service Intranet is built on these open standards, customers reap the benefits of cross-platform and cross-database support, flexibility, and vendor independence; they also gain the ability to leverage the innovation and products created by an entire industry, not just a single vendor.

As envisioned by Netscape, the Full Service Intranet provides four major user services:

> Information sharing and management
> Communication and collaboration
> Navigation
> Application access

The Full Service Intranet also provides four major network services:

> Directory
> Replication
> Security
> Management

URL F

Application access may be the most important intranet feature. The creation of the desktop PC has led to software decentralization. Persons my age are especially fond of the freedom from a central data processing center afforded by software decentralization. There is no doubt, however, that software costs have risen. The notion of recentralization of software with users accessing servers is a very interesting and important one, since it implies return of control to a central organization. Many companies prefer this control for other reasons. One reason is to prevent use of illegally copied software on company networks and hardware.

## PROTECTING THE WEB SITE

Your server needs protection — from power interruptions, on-site intruders, and Internet-based intruders. One standard admonition always seems to apply: back up; back up; back up; and then, don't forget to back up the material at the site. If you are running your own server, keep it under lock and key in a controlled access area. You have the same things to fear from permitting access to your server as you would have permitting access to your desktop computer, to your records, to your exams, and to your laboratories.

In my part of the world, violent thunderstorms are frequent and they lead to power outages that cause servers to go down. Perhaps it's not a smart thing to do, but I have my server software set to restart automatically such that when the computer restarts, the server software restarts. What to do in such a case is a big issue, not a small one. It is something you want to think about in advance of the event, not after it. As often as you've probably heard this in your lifetime about computers, it applies equally well for your server: back up; back up; back up; and then back up.

I've provided co-workers with access to my server using remote-control software (*Timbuktu,* Figure 13.1). I prefer to access the server directly when making software changes; my students do this from their homes.

> *Timbuktu*
>     Integrated networked remote control and remote access
>     Control or observe a remote Macintosh or PC
>     Connect to the network as a remote node using ARA
>     Works over LAN, WAN, the Internet, or dial-up
>     No matter where you are, or what you need to do, *Timbuktu Pro* for Networks is powerful networked remote, control software with built-in remote access. It's ideal for workgroups, remote workers, and help desk administrators. *Timbuktu Pro* is always ready to let you access corporate network resources, transfer files, remotely control other computers, collaborate, and so much more. It works over your LAN, WAN, the Internet, or over dial-up or ISDN lines to give you total LAN access, on demand.
>     Perfect for the remote worker.
>     Use *Timbuktu Pro* to make your job easier — whatever you need to do. For the business user, *Timbuktu Pro* lets you keep in touch from home, branch office, or on the road. You can control your desktop computer to retrieve files, draft documents, and create presentations — even work remotely with other users in real time to collaborate on projects. With the integrated ARA client, you can connect to the network as a remote node (requires ARA server for dial-up access), to read e-mail, log into file servers, and access other network services quickly and easily from a remote location.
>                                                              URL G

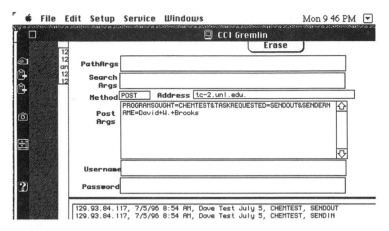

Figure 13.1. Screen capture from *Timbuktu*. *Timbuktu* was controlling the server in my office from another remote site in North America using a 14.4K modem.

In a sense, I think my approach to this problem may be asking for trouble. Many companies offer "firewalls" to keep intruders out. The following is a typical text:

> Internet connectivity is quickly becoming the norm for many organizations today. Without Email and remote access these organizations would find it difficult to survive in today's fast changing environment. Unfortunately the increase usage of the Internet has also included individuals who have less than honorable intentions. The need to secure and isolate your organization's network on today's Internet is more than a good idea; it's imperative.
>
> The GFX family of Internet firewall systems are designed to isolate and protect your internal network from unauthorized access. All members of the GFX family utilize the same software technology to provide protection. The members of the GFX family address different needs and performance.
>
>                                                                                            URL H

## CONTROLLING ACCESS; COURSE ENROLLMENT

It is a fairly straightforward matter to handle Web-based enrollment. This is much the same as selling something over the Web. I've used some *Hyper-Card*-based software to gather individual student data in my classes for nearly a decade, and converting that package to a Web-base was straightforward for me. There have been thousands of correspondence courses offered over the world in recent years. Many of the same problems and solutions encountered in correspondence courses apply to Web-teaching of for-credit courses.

With *WebStar* software, controlling server access is an easy matter. Protected materials are stored in folders, and the character sequence of the folder's name indicates to the software that a user name and password must be submitted by the user in order to permit access. Look for many ways of controlling access to servers emerging in new products, either in third-party add-ons or completely new server software.

On the Internet, you usually attempt to make all site information accessible to everyone. Plug-ins and helper applications are made freely available and downloadable. For an intranet, a different philosophy prevails. Some universities and companies will adopt an intranet approach to software licensing and control of access. Expect to see several strategies to emerge for this. At my institution we use *KeyServer* software. This software keeps track of the number of copies we're licensed to use concurrently. Each user has most of the program on their machine. When the software starts up, it goes out on our net to find the key server and, if a copy is available, the server sends back a "key" that permits use of the software. The number of copies available for use on the local network is reduced by one. Once the user quits that software, the number of copies available increases by one. In this system, a problem arises when a copy is left running that a user no longer needs; the system depends on user courtesy for success. Key servers are generic solutions to the software licensing problem. Expect to see proprietary solutions emerging, too. Also, don't forget the Weblets discussed in Chapter 12 as a solution to protecting local faculty authorship rights.

## EXAMS (ASSESSMENTS)

Taking exams over the WWW is possible. Expect to see fully electronic verifications emerging. At Rockefeller University, the U.S. Navy has sponsored the development of software (*FaceIt*) used to verify identification (Figure 13.2). Visible and infrared versions are available. From a video image captured either knowingly or surreptitiously, an individual is compared with a library of images confirming his or her identification. This method is used to control access to military computers, and may be used to control access to ships.

Another application is in bank security. In this situation, pictures are taken of customers and others, including thieves. From the images, a subsequent match becomes possible. That is, one can know with very high accuracy that a suspect is the same individual for whom one has video. The infrared system is alleged to be excellent; no amount of disguise seems to fool it.

Expect to see many approaches applied to computer testing. Certainly, when the site is controlled, it can be used for purposes of licensure, SAT tests, and so forth. I expect the same system used by you for videoconferencing to provide automatic identity verification — so that students can take secured ex-

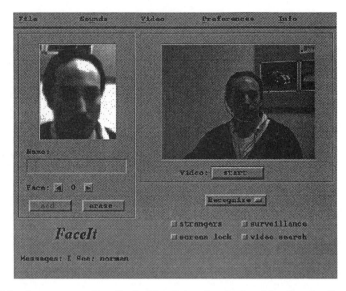

Figure 13.2.  Screen capture from Rockefeller University site describing *FaceIt* software.

ams 24 hours per day.  How you'll prevent collaboration, use of two computers, and similar problems related to performance remain open.  I suspect that just having verification possible throughout an exam period will be adequate.  Myself, I would always want to use the human verification after the fact.  Were I managing 1000 students in general chemistry, I might not feel this way.  Suppose you want to videoconference with students, one objective being verification of their content knowledge. Two hundred fifty hours of verification would be required assuming each session lasts only 15 minutes.  (That number tells us something about teaching that many students!)

As for the exams themselves, my sense is that having a powerful system can make it possible to use the practice tests and the real tests interchangeably. For some areas, the practice bank can be made so large that, with computer randomness about specific details included, learning the material is far easier than learning some strategies for just passing test items with little or no content knowledge.

I've adopted the philosophy that I'll use an independent verification procedure.  For example, I'll use one videoconference during which I talk to the student to verify his or her level of performance.  From this I'll validate an entire term of work.  For some courses, I'll use portfolio grading.  In this approach, students receive copies of the materials they used to complete successfully a course requirement, and some evaluation of both the student and the materials will detect nearly all falsification (cheating).

# CHAPTER 14

---

# LECTURING; MULTIMEDIA CLASSROOMS

This chapter encourages you to convert your classroom presentations into Web-ready formats, and includes practical suggestions about developing multimedia classrooms. It has little to do with actual use of the WWW. Putting your multimedia materials into WWW formats is a very good approach for making classroom presentations. It has the advantage that, should you choose to do so, you can make some or all of those materials directly available to students over the WWW.

Lecturing definitely has a poor reputation among many teachers. Certainly, when active learning is known to be more powerful than passive learning, lecturing is not usually a first-choice teaching strategy. When lecturers are very good, and other formal contacts with learning don't exist (i.e., there are no related laboratories or recitations), the structure lecturers provide for learners who have poor self-regulation skills may provide them with what it takes to survive.

In areas where opinions and points of view don't carry much weight, the lecture can be a very efficient mode of presentation. A wonderful lecturer in introductory chemistry from an excellent department once told me that the lecturer "sets the pace and tells the students what parts of the book they're not responsible for." The more I learn about instruction, the more I think this is an excellent view of what goes on in the classroom. The lecturer can clarify points and can broaden the view far beyond that possible from a textbook. I think this is what Schraw would call "providing structure."

When it comes right down to it, lecturing isn't all that bad. A teacher can do better than to lecture, but the necessary resources to do much better rarely are in place. The motivational aspect of face-to-face teaching often is underplayed or even ignored. For experts in an audience, lecture can be a very effective means of teaching. Dare I say this, I've even walked away from some lectures in my life feeling inspired. (I've also, on occasion, walked away very nearly expired.)

## AN OLDER MULTIMEDIA COURSE

As I noted in Chapter 3, my career as a chemistry lecturer involved ever increasing use of multimedia content. It began with lecture demonstrations (few in number) and movies (mostly from the *Chem Study* series). As time went on, there were more demonstrations. As I noted earlier, I once "canned" all of the prelaboratory instruction in a very large multisection course (with about 75 sections) just to deal with a vexing personnel problem. Television was used for the first semester, and synchronized slide–tape programs for the second semester.

Ultimately I was teaching all five lecture sections of 200+ students each in a large course using multimedia entirely [Brooks, 1985]. The course was difficult to organize, but rather simple to execute. All of the new lecture content was presented using synchronized, lap–dissolve, slide–tape programs. Prepared class notes allowed students to break down the material into coherent bundles (modules). There were occasional movies, all of which were transferred to videotape. There were many small-scale live demonstrations that were broadcast over a television system in the lecture room — the image of a penny (U.S. coin) could be made to fill each of six 25-inch television monitors. The demonstrations often were spectacular on the screen. For example, a penny heated to glowing red and immersed in the vapors of certain chemicals continues to glow red as it catalyzes the burning of the vapor on the penny surface. There were in-class experiments where data were recorded — and analyzed on the following day for all five sections gathering data the first day. There was a televised bulletin board that greeted students as they entered the lecture hall. There was cooperative learning — students were asked to work with neighbors on specific tasks. The only days in this course that were tiring for me were the days (five of them) before hour exams during which no new material was introduced and all I did was respond to student questions. That was very tiring; there was no time to rest. When canned material was introduced, 15–30 minutes worth per 50-minute period, I could relax.

Many things made this course work. In fact, it was very successful — the most popular among the required introductory science courses at UNL. First, the presentations were home grown, but they still were well done. The presentations were available on videotape — in a resource room — which students could access for review on demand. That room was open during all business hours and many evening hours every week. It was staffed by teaching assistants, too.

*None* of the chemical demonstrations were "canned." I felt that I wanted that experience to be live. Small as the experiments were, the lecture hall often would fill with some aroma, or there would be some other sensory event the emotional aspects of which could not be captured.

All of the old course exams going back six semesters were available on microfiche which the students obtained together with their class notes. At the time, a $0.15 fiche held an entire semester of exams (five hourlies, five repeat-hourlies, and a final). Second to the TAs, the microfiche readers were the most popular game in town. Worked-out exams have an excellent history as instructional devices. Instructors and top students usually feel that "new" exams are very similar to old ones, but struggling students often feel that "new" exams are unfair, and unlike the preceding semester's exam.

Setting up the multimedia course required $125,000. It was labor intensive; there were people who did nothing but make slides day after day. In fact, doing so *increased* rather than decreased the total time I spent on creating materials. Assistants would introduce errors such that I'd have to find theirs as well as my own.

## A MODERN MULTIMEDIA COURSE

Today the course described above could be managed in an entirely different manner. Classroom presentations could be handled today by a top-quality presentation program, such as *Astound, Persuasion, PowerPoint*, or *DeltaGraph Pro*. No dedicated support staff are needed. A spell checker is built in, so much of the extra time spent checking materials would be eliminated.

Today I would not choose this approach even though many of my faculty colleagues using multimedia have done so. I'd go directly to WWW formats — with an eye toward reducing the number of in-class presentations. (You can capture screens from presentation programs and put them on the Web, but I'd use straight text files with embedded images and hypertext.) Remember, when displaying such materials to a class, use a large-sized font.

In my version of a contemporary course, *all* of the lecture material would be converted to WWW formats. Everything. Any live lectures would be spun onto videotape directly from views of the WWW screens and these would be overlaid with sound. All of the media effects used in the old course — and there were many — would be incorporated into WWW multimedia.

For in-classroom material, I would keep most of the chemical demonstrations live. I think I would use live demonstrations as the theme — and I'd be sure that sights and smells would abound (within the limits set by OSHA, of course).

## POINTS OF DEPARTURE

Up to this point, all that has been suggested represents the conversion of a traditional lecture course to a multimedia course. You can stop there. I wouldn't. The screen material played in class, without sound, would be put up on the Web. I'm not completely sure whether I'd put the entire course on the Web at once, or put it up in synchrony with the lecture schedule. I'd probably put it up all at once, and encourage testing out of the course. (Yes, students successfully testing out *would* miss the live chemical demonstrations.)

The exams all would be on-line via the WWW, repeatable, self-scheduled, with rewards/penalties attached to deadlines. There probably would be two deadline dates — an extra point or two for finishing before the first one, and harsh, daily penalties for each day missed past the second one.

If I were teaching with TAs, they would be expected to use computers to maintain office hours — including some at night and over weekends. They would have the option of holding these office hours from their homes. Both hardware and Internet access for the TAs would be provided by the university. (If I were teaching at any university that was nonresidential in nature, I certainly would be looking toward instituting this kind of "after-hours" help.) I think I'd use software like *RoundTable* or *ChitChat* to support this assistance.

The curriculum would change drastically, too, with very substantial emphasis placed on the use of computer tools such as those that accomplish stoichiometry automatically. That's a different matter for a different book. Mine would still be a lecture course, but it would not look much like anything you see today. It would cost the university *less* to set up and run than did the course of 15 years ago. Why? Because today one can transfer the cost of the hardware and software and Internet hookups to the student! I currently am running graduate courses this way today, but these have much smaller enrollments than did my general chemistry classes.

In chemistry, I would go so far as to put parts of the lab course into kits, and have about half of the lab conducted at home or in the dormitory. Lab costs would go up, not down, because of the hardware needs for classes at off-campus environments. Overall, the costs of the course wouldn't change much. We did very well with our approach 15 years ago; I'm confident we'd do even better today.


## MULTIMEDIA IN THE GENERIC CLASSROOM

The scenario described above requires an equipped room. The large lecture room of 15 years ago included a large chemistry demonstration table and a system for TV distribution throughout that room. The lecture room environment needs to be changed so that it is *easy* for the lecturer to accomplish multimedia goals, and *easy* for the students to make use of the multimedia environment.

I first began lecturing from a computer in early 1988. It was a big deal. I had to carry my own liquid-crystal display (LCD), my computer (a Macintosh SE, appropriately wired for an LCD), and a suitable overhead projector that at once put out lots of light but was, nevertheless, cool. (LCD panels are usually very heat sensitive, and older overhead projectors run hot.) I had my own power strips and extension cords and lamps (to see with in a darkened room).

## SMART CARTS

In the first serious attempt made to put UNL into a modern multimedia world, we constructed "Smart Carts" (Figure 14.1). Smart Carts roll around from room to room, and they need some scheduling. Also, because many persons access them, they have software messiness problems and hard-drive clutter. When compared with my early days of computer-based multimedia, however, they are wonderful.

Our Smart Carts start out with the most powerful computer available. We purchase the largest hard drive, and extra RAM. We began in 1991, when a gigabyte and 16 Megabytes of RAM were a big deal. The computer output was pushed through to a color LCD panel. This same panel could take, as sources, a videotape player or a videodisk player. There were three image sources for the LCD. There was an enhanced sound system, capable of deafening levels. There was a 128-megabyte optical drive (a rewritable technology, slower than others but less subject to accidental losses), and, before extensive campus wiring, it was this gadget that kept our **sneakernet\*** going. The cart could be connected to whatever network was available. Today that is ethernet to a **TCP/IP\*** connection. Our first cart is still in use, even though it has seen such extensive use by faculty that the legs are literally falling down. It's been used *very* heavily. Smart Carts need to be on the same floor as the classrooms where they are used. They don't take well to elevators, and they are particularly prone to misbehave when taken out of doors between buildings.

Figure 14.1.  The first UNL Teachers College Smart Cart.

## Networked Resources

You will create courseware materials in your office, laboratory, or some media production center. You'll present them in a classroom. Somehow, you've got to be able to move the information. In the days of sneakernet, you'd just push the information onto a floppy and carry it in your pocket. Our Smart Carts included 3.5-inch optical drives. Today we would use Zip drives. The *best* thing for you to have is networked access from the machines where you create or store your materials to the machines where you present and teach. Hard-wired networking has been one of the biggest improvements in my efficiency and use of media materials.

## Display Devices

There are at least three choices for a display system. You can make use of an existing television system with its hanging or standing monitors (Figure 14.2). This is probably the least expensive system. The room can be lighted fully, and students can take notes easily.

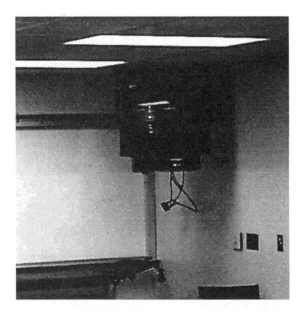

Figure 14.2. Hanging monitors remain an option. If you don't have monitors, then conversion from the computer RGB to a video signal (like NTSC) is required, and there will be a substantial diminution in image quality.

Using an existing television system throws away a good deal of the intrinsic resolution available, however, and this is a major drawback. Monitors of appropriate size for classrooms are very heavy, and pushing two or more of them from room to room can be a serious imposition on a teacher, too.

In order to drive an ordinary TV monitor, you need something that converts the signal meant for your RGB monitor (computer monitor) to a video signal (NTSC). These devices cost a few hundred dollars. Test them in place before you buy! TelevEyes (Digital Vision, Inc.) "converts your computer's VGA signal to recordable NTSC video. Not only can you record your computer's display on a VCR, but you can view it simultaneously on any standard TV monitor."

Projection systems are highly desirable but also the most expensive solution. Ceiling-mounted projectors stay in place (Figure 14.3); portable projectors are available (Figure 14.4). The room may need to be significantly darkened. Projector costs have come down, and their maintenance (tuning) has been simplified. All in all, however, this probably is the best, most teacher-friendly solution.

Figure 14.3. At my institution there is an increasing use of ceiling projectors.

An incandescent lamp system with controlled output is extremely helpful in all multimedia rooms regardless of the image projection system.

The third option, LCDs, also is improving with time. They can be used in situations almost the same as an ordinary overhead projector. (Most do cut way down on the available transmitted light.) Putting an LCD on a Smart Cart may be, all in all, the most workable compromise solution. As soon as you start to look at the option of installing video systems in two or more rooms, LCDs become the least expensive solution.

Figure 14.4. We use a Portable Sharp Projector for many situations. This device is rented by the Instructional Design Center at a rate of $75/day, and is in use 5–10 hours per week. It is an excellent institutional selection for situations where LCDs are inappropriate. The devices are very portable. Although costly, they are still less so than permanently mounted devices.

## Computers

It has been our policy to put the biggest and best computer of the chosen platform in a multimedia room. In some rooms, we've placed the best available Macintosh, Wintel, *and* NeXT computers. This has proven to be one of our wiser policies. Smart Carts end up being platform specific. If you have extra resources, think first of extra RAM and next of a large hard drive. Always, plan on connection to a network so that the teacher can download the materials from her or his personal desk to the teaching computer. As noted earlier, this means wiring both teachers' offices and classrooms.

## Videotape

Nearly all disciplines have valuable video resources available. Also, in the United States, nearly all of these play from an NTSC video standard in VHS format. It makes sense, therefore, to include VHS playback capabilities in any system you might develop to enhance lecturing.

What quality should you pay for? That's very difficult to say. The most important criterion is that you be able to feed the video image into the same projection system you're using for the computer. While quality video replay equipment is a good idea, using a tape player that can be computer controlled probably is excessive in all but a very few special cases.

## Videodisk

Very few multimedia developers are making videodisks these days. However, there are many videodisks available in the sciences, particularly biology and chemistry, on which powerful visual databases are available. Videodisks offer random access and, if teachers intend to use them, having systems that offer random access to frames and chapters on the videodisk is valuable. A videodisk can, in principle, hold as many as 54,000 images. Some biology databases do contain thousands of images. Find a videodisk player that permits computer control. In the Macintosh world, many are available that can be connected from the computer to the videodisk player through the (modem) serial port. For example, Pioneer's CLD-V2800 LaserDisc Player includes an RS-232 port.

## In-Class Video Stands

Made famous by the Simpson murder trial is the television projection stand. ELMOs are one such stand. The ELMO Web page listed five models of "Visual Presenters" in October 1996. Video camera stands are useful tools for demonstrating — objects and books, both (Figure 14.5).

## SEATING ARRANGEMENTS

There is much less variation in lecture hall than lab layouts. In lecture, you might want to think about a design that minimizes the distance between teacher and students. This means that short and fat is preferred over long and lean. (Imagine a rectangle. The teacher wants to be placed near the middle of a long side, if possible.)

Student-in-control is, in general, a successful model for learning. This means that you need ways for students to access materials. The time-honored approach to this is to have the students in a school-managed computer laboratory. The way you design your computer labs for students will impact on the kind of learning environment you maintain. If your computers are arranged in rows, then students climb into position and hunker down (Figure 14.6). Other arrangements actually promote student exchanges more, and also facilitate teacher access. We favor the hexagonal arrangement shown (Figure 14.7). It has worked very well in all of the laboratories where we have tried it. All in all, we seem to accommodate nearly as many students as we might in the linear arrangements.

Figure 14.5. A video projector stand (Canon RE 600 MK 11 Video Visualizer). A very useful tool for teaching many disciplines, the projector is shown here displaying a flowering plant.

Figure 14.6. Traditional arrangement of computers in rows, with 40 independent stations, all connected generically to the building network and all Web accessible. This is a university-sponsored community or open laboratory maintained in the Teachers College. This lab rarely is used for teaching.

## THE MULTIMEDIA CLASSROOM

Our campus today is creating dozens of multimedia classrooms. Some of these are large (200–250 seats), while others are more modest in size (30–50 seats). We do tend to convert the big classrooms where large, introductory

Figure 14.7. The "New Media Classroom" at the University of Nebraska showing four hexagonal pods (24 student stations and an instructor station), a very desirable arrangement that encourages student/student exchanges and facilitates faculty observation. An adjacent Teachers College lab has three hexagonal pods. Both labs are used heavily for interactive teaching, day and night.

courses are taught. The biggest advantage of these rooms is that the hardware is stored in a locked cabinet. Finding a simple, single system that permits control of all of the hardware simultaneously is a challenge. Many faculty undertrain and get stuck just before class. Sometimes the systems are fragile, and need lots of tender loving care during frequent maintenance periods. Once a faculty member has been burned in a multimedia room, he or she tends to drop out. About half of the burned faculty users drop out on our campus; wooing them back to multimedia use is a challenge.

## WHAT NOT TO DO

Control is one of the biggest issues faced when designing a room. Who has control: staff in charge of the room; the teachers; the students? A friend of mine with good technology skills was asked to teach two sections of a course in technical communications, one on each of two campuses. He planned all sorts of student interactions including using e-mail, creating HTML pages, and using presentation programs. He often tried to use supporting media in class, such as videotapes.

On one campus, as a result of room design and in spite of 4 hours of training, he had great difficulty in performing such simple tasks as showing videotapes. There were just too many power switches located in different places that needed to be turned on. When he tried to give students access to the same software he had at his terminal (this is a lab with about 30 student stations equipped with powerful computers), campus policy forbade student use of the same programs. That campus licensed software for use on individual machines, while the other one used a key server. With a key server, all machines can have a nearly functional copy of all licensed software, but, once the number of licenses available is in use, the key server will not serve keys to additional machines. Under a key server system, it is rude to keep software running when not in use because that prevents other potential users from access. For the teacher to make software instruction work, he would need to hold class in different student laboratories on the other campus. On that campus, achieving all of these goals was no problem.

He became rather discouraged. When operating in one environment, teaching is straight forward, while in the other, it presents too many barriers. As many others, he stopped trying to use technology in his teaching.

Overall, my own experience with classroom teaching using technology seems to be getting better and better. In 1988, I had to lug low-quality hardware into every room where I intended technology use. Today I usually can find an excellent room to teach my classes, even one where my students also have powerful computers. I see this aspect of teaching as improving steadily on my campus and on most other campuses as well. Using a campus network, I can move material from my office to the classroom site. The most difficult step usually is finding an open time to test the software before class.

Lecturing is probably a better teaching technique than current ratings of techniques would suggest these days. Multimedia lecturing using Web software is relatively easy and powerful. If you've not wet your feet yet, this is a comfortable and personally rewarding place to start. Who knows, after a few years it may grow on you so much that you compete to become your departmental Webmaster!

# REFERENCES

Abraham, M. (1996). Personal communication.

The American Heritage Talking Dictionary (The American Heritage Dictionary of the English Language). Cambridge, MA: SoftKey International, Inc.

Ansorge, C. J., & Wilhite, M. S. (1994). Multimedia Instruction: Student and Faculty Perceptions. Office of the Senior Vice Chancellor for Academic Affairs, University of Nebraska–Lincoln.

Barrie, J. M., & Presti, D. E. (1996). The World Wide Web as an Instructional Tool. *Science, 274*, 371–372.

Bertini, M. (1986). Some Implications of Field Dependence for Education. In M. Bertini, L. Pizzamiglio, & S. Wapner (Eds.), *Field Dependence* (pp. 93–106). Hillsdale, NJ: Lawrence Erlbaum Associates.

Borg, W. R., & Gall, M. D. (1989). *Educational Research* (5th ed.). New York: Longman.

Borkowski, J. G., Chan, L. K. S., & Muthukrishna, N. (1997, in press). A Process-Oriented Model of Metacognition: Links between Motivation and Executive Functioning. In G. Schraw (Ed.), *Issues in the Measurement of Metacognition*. Lincoln, NE: Buros–Nebraska Press.

Boschmann, E. (Ed.). (1995). *The Electronic Classroom*. Medford, NJ: Learned Information, Inc.

Brooks, D. W. (1985). Live Chemistry; Canned Lectures. *Journal of College Science Teaching, 15*, 110.

Brooks, D. W. (1994a). Stoichiometer. *Computers in Chemical Education Newsletter* (Spring), 6–10.

Brooks, D. W. (1994b). *Stoichiometer*. Lincoln, NE: Synaps. SYNAPS@ LTEC.NET

Bruning, R. (1996). Personal communication. Discussion of role of site leaders in Japanese course.

Bruning, R., Landis, M., Hoffman, E., & Grosskopf, K. (1993). Perspectives on an Interactive Satellite-Based Japanese Language Course. *The American Journal of Distance Education, 7*(3), 22–38.

Cassanova, J. (1996). Computers in the Classroom — What Works and What Doesn't. *Computers in Chemical Education Newsletter* (Spring), 5–9.

Cassanova, J., & Cassanova, S. L. (1991). Computer as Electronic Blackboard: Remodeling the Organic Chemistry Lecture. Educom Review, 26, 31.

Chapman, O., Russell, A. A., & Wegner, P. (1996). The Molecular Science Curriculum on the Net. *Abstracts, 14th Biennial Conference on Chemical Education.* Clemson, SC: Division of Chemical Education, ACS.

Clark, R. E. (1982). Antagonism between Achievement and Enjoyment in ATI Studies. *Educational Psychologist, 17*, 92–101.

Clark, R. E. (1983). Reconsidering Research on Learning from Media. *Review of Educational Research, 53*, 445–459.

Clark, R. E. (1995a). Media Will Never Influence Learning. *Educational Technology Research and Development, 42*(2), 21–29.

Clark, R. E. (1995b). Media and Method. *Educational Technology Research and Development, 42*(3), 7–10.

Clark, R. E., & Salomon, G. (1986). Media in Teaching. In M. C. Wittrock (Ed.), *Handbook of Research on Teaching* (pp. 464–478). New York: Macmillan.

Cooley, L. A. (1995). Evaluating the Effects on Conceptual Understanding and Achievement of Enhancing and Introductory Calculus Course with a Computer Algebra System. Ph.D. Dissertation, New York University.

Crick, F. (1994). *The Astonishing Hypothesis.* New York: Charles Scribner's Sons.

Drucker, P. F. (1977). *People and Performance: The Best of Peter Drucker on Management* (pp. 151–155). New York: Harper & Row.

Dugdale, S., Thompson, P. W., Harvey, W., Demana, F., Waits, B. K., Kieran, C., McConnell, J. W., & Christmas, P. (1995). Technology and Algebra Curriculum Reform: Current Issues, Potential Directions, and Research Questions. *Journal of Computers in Mathematics and Science Teaching, 14*(3), 325–355.

Dwight, J. & Erwin, M. (1996). *Using CGI.* Indianapolis, IN: Que Publishing.

Eaton, J. (1996, Nov. 11). PNG graphics format gaining Web support. *MacWeek*, pp. 22–24.

Ellis, A., & Fouts, J. (1993). *Research on Education Innovations*. New York: Eye on Education.

Enger, J., Toms-Wood, A., & Cohn, K. (1978). Evaluation of a Videocassette-Discussion Teaching Format in General Chemistry. *Journal of Chemical Education*, *55*(4), 230–232.

Engst, A. C. (1995). *Internet Starter Kit*. Indianapolis, IN: Hayden Books.

Flowers, J. H., & Hauer, T. (1995). Musical versus Visual Graphs: Cross Modal Equivalence in Perception of Time Series Data. *Human Factors*, *37*, 553–559.

Gabel, D. (1995). Science. In G. Cawelti (Ed.), *Handbook of Research on Improving Student Achievement* (pp. 123–143). Arlington, VA: Educational Research Service.

Gardner, H. (1983; 1993). *Frames of Mind*. New York: Basic Books.

Gelder, J. I. (1994). *ChemAnimations*. Lincoln, NE: Synaps. SYNAPS@ LTEC.NET

Glider, W. (1996). Personal communication.

Graham, I. S. (1996). *The HTML Sourcebook* (2nd ed.). New York: Wiley.

Greenbowe, T. J. (1983). An Investigation of Variables Involved in Chemistry Problem Solving. Doctoral Dissertation, Purdue University.

Greenbowe, T. J. (1996). Relation between Field Independence and Effect of Multimedia Materials. Personal communication. (Submitted for publication).

Grouws, D. A. (1995). Mathematics. In G. Cawelti (Ed.), *Handbook of Research on Improving Student Achievement* (pp. 97–109). Arlington, VA: Educational Research Service.

Haight, G. P. Jr. (1978). Teaching a Large Introductory Chemistry course Using T. V. Cassettes. *Journal of Chemical Education*, *55*(4), 221–224.

Hannafin, M. J., & Hooper, S. R. (1993). Learning Principles, in Fleming, M., & Levie, W. H. (Eds.) *Instructional Message Design* (2nd ed.) (pp. 191–231). Englewood Cliffs, NJ: Educational Technology Publications.

Harasim, L., Hiltz, S. R., Teles, L., & Turoff, M. (1995). *Learning Networks*. Cambridge, MA: MIT Press.

Hayes, D. P., Wolfer, L. T., & Wolfe, M. F. (1996). Schoolbook Simplification and Its Relation to the Decline in SAT-Verbal Scores. *American Educational Research Journal*, *33*(2), 489–508.

Heinich, R., Molenda, M., Russell, J. D., & Smaldino, S. E. (1996). *Instructional Media and Technologies for Learning* (5th ed.) Englewood Cliffs: Prentice–Hall.

Herron, J. D. (1996). *The Chemistry Classroom: Formulas for Successful Teaching*. Washington, DC: American Chemical Society.

Hiltz, S. R. (1988). A Virtual Classroom on E. I. E. S. (Research report No. 25). Center for Computerized Conferencing and Communication, New Jersey Institute of Technology.

Hiltz, S. R. (1994). *The Virtual Classroom: Learning Without Limits via Computer Networks*. Norwood, NJ: Ablex Publishing Corp.

Horn, C. A. (1993). An Exploration of the Effects of General Ability, Mastery Goal Orientation, Self-Efficacy, and Elaborative Strategy Use on Student Achievement and Construction of Domain Knowledge in Introductory Biology. Ph.D. Dissertation, University of Nebraska–Lincoln.

Horn, C. (1995). Seminar on Student Performance in Large Biology Classes. Personal communication.

Horn, C., Bruning, R., Schraw, G., Curry, E., & Katkanant, C. (1993). Paths to Success in the College Classroom. *Contemporary Educational Psychology*, *18*, 464–478.

Jonassen, D. H., Campbell, J. P., & Davidson, M. E. (1995). Learning *with* Media: Restructuring the Debate. *Educational Technology Research and Development*, *42*(2), 31–39.

Keller, F. S., & Sherman, J. G. (1974). *PSI, the Keller Plan Handbook: Essays on a Personalized System of Instruction*. Menlo Park, CA: Benjamin.

Klein, T. J. (1993). A Comparative Study on the Effectiveness of Differential Equations Instruction With and Without a Computer Algebra System (Algebra). Ed.D. Dissertation, Peabody College for Teachers of Vanderbilt University.

Kotz, J. C., & Vining, W. J. (1996). *Saunders Interactive General Chemistry CD-ROM*. Fort Worth, TX: Saunders College Publishing.

Kozma, R. B. (1995a). Will Media Influence Learning? Reframing the Debate. *Educational Technology Research and Development*, *42*(2), 7–19.

Kozma, R. B. (1995b). A Reply: Media and Methods. *Educational Technology Research and Development*, *42*(3), 11–14.

Lavin, S. J. (1995). Personal communication. Population change in Nebraska counties, 1900 to 1990. Map animation. Department of Geography, University of Nebraska–Lincoln.

Liu, D. (1996). Teaching Chemistry on the Internet. Ph.D. Dissertation, University of Nebraska–Lincoln. (http://www.cci.unl.edu/CVs/Dissertations/ liuDiss.html)

MacEachren, A. M., & Monmonier, M. (1992). Introduction. *Cartography and Geographic Information Systems, 19*(4), 197–200.

McLuhan, M. (1964). *Understanding Media: The Extensions of Man.* New York: McGraw-Hill.

Meyers, C., & Jones, T. B. (1993). *Promoting Active Learning.* San Francisco: Jossey–Bass.

Moore, J. W., Brooks, D. W., Fuller, R. G., & Jensen, D. D. (1977). Repeatable Testing. *Journal of Chemical Education, 54,* 276.

Morgan, M., Wandling, J., & Casselberry, R. (1996). *Webmaster Expert Solutions.* Indianapolis, IN: Que Corporation.

Morrison, G. R. (1995). The Media Effects Question: "Unresolvable" or Asking the Right Question. *Educational Technology Research and Development, 42*(2), 41–44.

Norem, J. K., & Cantor, N. (1986). Defensive Pessimism: Harnessing Anxiety as Motivation. *Journal of Personality and Social Psychology, 51,* 1208–1217.

Norman, D. A. (1991). Cognitive Artifacts. In J. M. Carroll (Ed.), *Designing Interaction* (pp. 17–38). Cambridge: Cambridge University Press.

Park, K. (1993). A Comparative Study of the Traditional Calculus Course vs. the Calculus & *Mathematica* Course (CAI, Calculus, & *Mathematica*). Ph.D. Dissertation, University of Illinois at Urbana–Champaign.

Pence, H. E. (1993). Combining Cooperative Learning and Multimedia in General Chemistry. *Education, 113*(3), 375–380.

Pinker, S. (1994). *The Language Instinct.* New York: Morrow.

Pintrich, P. R. (1995). Understanding Self-Regulated Learning. In P. R. Pintrich (Ed.), *Understanding Self-Regulated Learning* (pp. 3–12). San Francisco: Jossey–Bass.

Pintrich, P. R., & Schunk, D. H. (1996). *Motivation in Education.* Englewood Cliffs, NJ: Merrill (Prentice–Hall).

Piper, W. (retold by) (1984; 1930). *The Little Engine That Could.* New York: Platt & Munk.

Pittenger, D. J. (1993). The Utility of the Myers–Briggs Type Indicator. *Review of Educational Research, 63*, 467–488.

Porzio, D. T. (1994). The Effects of Differing Technological Approaches to Calculus on Students' Use and Understanding of Multiple Representations When Solving Problems (Problem Solving). Ph.D. Dissertation, The Ohio State University.

Pressley, M., with McCormick, C. B. (1995). *Advanced Educational Psychology for Educators, Researchers, and Policy Makers.* New York: Harper Collins.

Reiser, R. A. (1995). Clark's Invitation to the Dance: An Instructional Designer's Response. *Educational Technology Research and Development, 42*(2), 45–48.

Ritchey, T. (1996). *Programming JavaScript for Netscape 2.0.* Indianapolis, IN: New Riders Publishing.

Ross, S. M. (1995a). Delivery Trucks or Groceries? More Food for Thought on Whether Media (Will, May, Can't) Influence Learning. *Educational Technology Research and Development, 42*(2), 5–6.

Ross, S. M. (1995b). From Ingredients to Recipes ... and Back: It's the Taste That Counts. *Educational Technology Research and Development, 42*(3), 5–6.

Sawrey, B. A. (1996). Computers in Introductory Chemistry Courses: Simple to Sophisticated. *Abstracts 14th Biennial Conference on Chemical Education.* Clemson, SC: Division of Chemical Education, ACS.

Schank, R. C., & Cleary, C. (1995). *Engines for Education.* Hillsdale, NJ: Lawrence Erlbaum Associates.

Schraw, G. (1994). The Effect of Metacognitive Knowledge on Local and Global Monitoring. *Contemporary Educational Psychology, 19*, 143–154.

Schwartz, J. (1995). Where is the Voice of the Author? In *Creating Effective Multimedia and Assessing Its Impact.* MIT: Center for Educational Computing Initiatives.

Seyer, P. (1991). *Understanding Hypertext.* Blue Ridge Summit, PA: Windcrest Books (McGraw–Hill).

Shapiro, E. S. (1984). Self-Monitoring Procedures. In T. H. Ollendick & M. Hersen (Eds.), *Child Behavior Assessment: Principles and Procedures* (pp. 148-165). New York: Pergamon Press.

Shrock, S. A. (1995). The Media Influence Debate: Read the Fine Print, But Don't Lose Sight of the Big Picture. *Educational Technology Research and Development, 42*(2), 49–53.

Smith, S. G., & Jones, L. L. (1989). Images, Imagination, and Chemical Reality. *Journal of Chemical Education, 66*, 8–11.

Sternberg, R. J. (1994). Allowing for Thinking Styles. *Educational Leadership, 52*(3), 36–40.

Sternberg, R. J. (1996). Myths, Countermyths, and Truths About Intelligence. *Educational Researcher, 25*(2), 11–16.

Streeter, A. (1996a, June 24). Leave the doors open, but keep the information secure. *MacWeek*, p. 33–34

Streeter, A. (1996b, August 26). Users build a CAD arsenal: Best of breed vs. all-in-one. *MacWeek*, p. 37–38.

Symons, S., Snyder, B. I., Cariglia-Bull, T., & Pressley, M. (1989). Why Be Optimistic About Cognitive Strategy Instruction? In C. B. McCormick, G. E. Miller, & M. Pressley (Eds.), *Cognitive Strategy Research* (pp. 1–32). Berlin: Springer-Verlag.

Tennyson, R. D. (1995). The Big Wrench vs. Integrated Approaches: The Great Media Debate. *Educational Technology Research and Development, 42*(3), 15–28.

Waits, B. K., & Demana, F. (1992). A Case Against Computer Symbolic Manipulation in School Mathematics Today. *The Mathematics Teacher, 85*(3), 180–183.

Walberg, H. J. (1995). Generic Practices. In G. Cawelti (Ed.), *Handbook of Research on Improving Student Achievement* (pp. 7–19). Arlington, VA: Educational Research Service.

Wells, R. A. (1990). Distributed Training for the Reserved Component: Remote Delivery Using Asynchronous Computer Conferencing (No. 2Q26374A794). Idaho National Engineering Laboratory, Idaho Falls, ID.

Wessel, T., Caffrey, F., & Gannon, J. (1996). A Custom-Made Multimedia Approach to Student Pre-Laboratory Preparation — Design, Implementation, and Evaluation. *Abstracts 14th Biennial Conference on Chemical Education*. Clemson, SC: Division of Chemical Education, ACS.

Williamson, V. M., & Abraham, M. R. (1995). The Effects of Computer Animation on the Particulate Mental Models of College Chemistry Students. *Journal of Research in Science Teaching, 32*(5), 521–534.

Witkin, H. A. (1949). Sex differences in perception. *Transactions of the New York Academy of Sciences, 12*, 22–26.

Witkin, H. A., Goodenough, D. R., & Karp, S. A. (1967). Stability of Cognitive Style from Childhood to Young Adulthood. *Journal of Personality and Social Psychology, 7*, 291–300.

Witkin, H. A., Oltman, P. K., Raskin, E., & Karp, S. A. (1971). *A Manual for the Embedded Figures Test*. Palo Alto, CA: Consulting Psychologists Press.

# GLOSSARY

active learning: learner speaks, writes, performs experiments, plans, etc., as opposed to reads, listens to lecture, etc.

animation: as used in *Web-Teaching*, a sequence of drawings or graphic images stitched together to form a movie.

applet: an application written in the Java language intended for inclusion within a Web page.

ASCII: a standard for handling plain text.

audiotutorial system: structured learning system in which audiotapes provide the instructions. Many other media may be involved.

bandwidth: in WWW jargon, the amount of electronic information that can be delivered per unit time.

bookmark: in WWW jargon, a bookmark is a menu-accessible reference to a URL (Web site address) such that, when selected, your browser goes to the site with no typing required. Bookmarks speed access to Web sites.

browser: software used by the client or receiver on the WWW. Most of these have graphical user interfaces. Examples are Netscape *Navigator* and MS *Explorer*.

CAI: computer-aided instruction; computer-assisted instruction. Instruction where the rate of presentation and branches are determined by a computer (program) based on user performance.

CD-ROM: compact disk read-only memory. A storage medium. Once read only and slow, this medium is expected to become both read–write and much faster before the year 2000.

CGI: common gateway interface. Used by a server to process information received from a user (client, browser).

clickable image (map): image where clicking certain regions activates a hypertext link to a URL (Web address) and begins browser access to that address. The address may be some location within the currently viewed page.

clicking; click: to depress a (the) mouse button; depression of button on a mouse.

clipboard: temporary electronic storage area (used in Macintoshes for documents, text, pictures, sounds, etc.)

cognitive artifact: according to Donald Norman, a device created to assist with a task that changes in a fundamental way the skills needed to succeed with the task.

comprehensive multimedia delivery system: a delivery system capable of delivering nearly all media formats — text, sound, images, movies, etc.

compression; compressed file: file in which wasted space has been removed by using a computer application that replaces current bits and bytes with new ones. Formulas or algorithms allow duplicate or empty space removal, and also permit reconstruction of the original file identically (lossless compression) or nearly identically (lossy compression).

cookie: a line of text that may persist on the client side found in a file that, on a Macintosh, is in the Netscape folder of the Preferences folder (or equivalent). A cookie provides a mechanism for storing small amounts of information on the client computer.

digital camera: records image as digital information on some digital storage substrate (like a memory card).

digital technologies: technologies in which information is dealt with as strings of zeroes and ones rather than as a continuous (analog) signal.

domain name: name given to an IP address. The author's server has the domain name www.cci.unl.edu, which stands for a WWW server in the Center for Curriculum and Instruction at the University of Nebraska.

draw; drawing program: graphics program that creates image elements using vectors whose appearance can be modified by selection followed by changing a parameter. [Contrast with paint programs that store information on a pixel-by-pixel (dot-by-dot) basis.]

drive space: the amount of room available on a hard drive. At one time, PCs with 10-megabyte drives were thought to be huge; today 2-gigabyte drives (200 times more storage) are commonplace.

e-mail: electronic mail delivered and received over a digital network such as the Internet. Software creates, transmits, and interprets the data streams.

freeware: software created as a public service and provided without charge, often over the Internet (ftp, WWW).

ftp: file transfer protocol. A procedure for transferring files from one computer to another.

GIF: graphics interchange format. A pixel-based image format created by CompuServe and used widely on the WWW.

gopher: connects user to site with menus and text that can be downloaded. Once widely used, and still valuable for text, gophers largely have been supplanted by the WWW.

helper application: program used by a browser to assist with some task or operation. For example, *Navigator* uses the helper application *StuffIt Expander* to translate and expand hqx files.

HTML, HTML tag: hypertext markup language. The WWW involves sending files around the network in extremely simple formats so as to make them machine and platform independent. Inside these text files are "tags" read as text but demarked in such a way as to provide information to the software (browser) about how to display the text. This is not an exact method; the files may appear rather differently on different browsers.

http: hypertext transfer protocol. A procedure used by computers to transfer files from servers to clients (browsers). This is the principal procedure used on the WWW.

hypermedia: multimedia linked so as to permit branching from one place to another based on the intent of the user (or programmer).

hypertext: text linked so that the user can jump from one idea to another, usually by clicking on text.

Internet: a dynamic electronic network that permits computers connected anywhere on that network to exchange information. The Internet is essentially a worldwide network.

intranet: a network that uses the same software as used on the Internet but that has controlled access — often physically constrained to the wiring within an organization. A barrier allows some information to cross to the outside world, but much information exchange is confined exclusively within the organization.

IP address: a string of four numbers between 0 and 255 separated by periods. Each machine on the Internet is assigned a unique IP address (from among 4,294,967,296). The world is fast running out of these addresses because of the way they are assigned. The first two numbers define a domain — such as the University of Nebraska, and that is why numbers are becoming scarce.

Java: an object oriented programming language that strives for cross-platform interoperability. Java compliers create *bytecode* that can be used on all Java platforms. Each platform interprets Java bytecode.

JavaScript: very much like Java, JavaScript is intended for use within a WWW browser and can take advantage of browser features.

JPEG: standards for a lossy compression format used for images and *QuickTime* movies.

Kinkos: commercial supplier of information handling services centering on multimedia production and especially duplication services.

LCD (liquid crystal display): used in conjunction with overhead projectors, LCD panels offer a means of displaying computer screens to large audiences.

listserv: an automatic mailing system such that, when someone sends mail to the listserv, a copy is transmitted to all subscribers to that listserv.

lossless; lossy: descriptions of file compression strategies. Lossless compression retains all of the information so that the compressed file may be reconstructed exactly. Lossy compression involves some loss of information. JPEG and MPEG are lossy compression formats.

Macintosh: computer with a graphical user interface (GUI) first introduced in 1984 by Apple Computer.

map: a clickable image such that, if clicking occurs in a "hot spot," some action will be taken. On the WWW, this usually means activating some URL.

metaprinter: software that behaves like a printer by receiving encoded information but which converts that to a different format. In principle, any application printing to a metaprinter may have its output converted to an HTML-tagged file that will appear on a browser much as would the printed copy.

MIME: Multipurpose Internet Mail Extension. Standardized scheme that permits browser software to determine what to do with a file. The file is assigned an extension written as a few letters and a period or dot. Files ending in .html or .htm, for example, are interpreted as being tagged text. Files ending in .GIF are GIF image files, while those ending in .jpg or .jpeg are JPEG images. A file ending in .hqx has been encoded (in a format called BinHex 4.0) so that it can be transferred from computer to computer.

modem, 14.4K modem: a device that modulates computer signals before telephone transmission and demodulates telephone signals to computer signals. Permits transmission of digital information over telephone wires. Devices usually are described by the speed at which they transmit/receive bits of information (14.4K means 14,400 bits per second).

morph; morphing: metamorphosis of one image into another.

movie: in the context of this book, a computer file that may be played by a computer as if it were a motion picture.

MPEG: a lossy compression format that is very efficient for movies. Requires hardware (chip) to replay from most desktop computers.

multimedia: forms of media, such as video, audio, text, and images.

Myers–Briggs, MBTI: a very popular "type" inventory often used by teachers to suggest styles of learning or personality.

optical character recognition, OCR: a scheme for taking printed images as from typewriting, newspapers, and books, and converting those images of letters into digital text files usable by computers.

paint; painting program: image strategy involving individual dots or pixels in a screen. Difficult to modify after files are created.

.pdf: file extension for files created by *Adobe Acrobat*. These files may be opened using a freeware reader and provide a means for distributing documents with preserved format regardless of the word processor used to create them.

Photo CD: digital format developed by Kodak and used to create optical storage media holding very large amounts of visual information.

pixel: dot on a computer screen. There are typically 72 dots per inch on a computer screen.

plug-in: dynamic code modules, native to a specific platform on which a browser runs, that enhance the capabilities of the browser.

QuickTime: a system software solution developed by Apple computer to provide general approaches to presentation of time based materials such as audio, animations, and movies. Handles materials in JPEG and MPEG formats. Available for both Macintosh and Windows.

RAM: random-access memory. Space in computer where programs and data are stored while in use. At one time, 64K was large; this manuscript was produced on a system with 96 megabytes.

self-regulator (self-regulation): a learner who actively controls his or her learning by use of good strategies for cognition and motivation.

server: computer connected to the WWW that transmits files. Most computers can be made into servers given suitable software. *WebStar* can make nearly any Macintosh into a server.

shareware: software created as a public service and provided for testing after which, if used for substantial time (usually defined as a month), the user is honor bound to pay a small fee to the creator.

sneakernet: describes pseudonetwork where files are copied from drive to disk at one computer, and then transported (by mail, or perhaps someone walking wearing sneakers) to a different computer for copying from disk to drive.

spreadsheet: software to handle systematic arithmetic and logic operations. Originally created to help with bookkeeping operations. (Spreadsheets vaulted personal computers to the desktops of everyday business managers.)

tag: in HTML, an instruction embedded within an ordinary text file that may be interpreted by browser software as an instruction.

talking face: TV jargon for situation where video consists of closeup view of person speaking. Usually considered bad for TV and for instruction.

TCP/IP: transmission control protocol/Internet protocol. Procedures used by computer networks to exchange data.

UNIX: a powerful operating system found on many computers, particularly larger or mainframe computers.

URL; uniform resource locator: a four-part information string that conveys a type of operation (e.g., http, ftp, mailto), the IP address of a machine where the desired file is located, the path on that machine to the file, and the name of the file.

Webify: making material ready for delivery over the WWW.

weblet: a small and usually closed system of files that make use of Web software. Often used to deal with bandwidth or student control problems.

Web page: describes a hypertext file transmitted from server to client using the WWW.

Web site: server that serves the WWW. Usually indicates a net location from which a substantial amount of related information is served.

Web-teaching: instruction conducted using the WWW.

whiteboard: shared screen in which two (or more) parties can discuss a document and independently mark the same document.

Wintel: refers to hardware and software based on Microsoft Windows software and computer central processing chips manufactured by the Intel Corporation.

World Wide Web, WWW: a scheme for using the Internet to exchange information in hypermedia formats.

wrap: refers to text automatically going from one line to the next as more text is added. Typists once needed to type "carriage returns" to implement wrap. Wrap is an attribute to TEXTAREA form elements.

WYBMADIITY: will you buy me a drink if I tell you?  Often found on signs in establishments that sell alcoholic beverages.  (Just testing to see what you read.)

WYSIWYG: what you see is what you get.  An acronym suggesting that whatever appears on the screen will appear the same when printed.

# SOFTWARE LIST

A list of software that has been found to be useful by me or has come highly recommended by co-workers or reliable magazines follows. I've tried nearly all of these programs on the Macintosh side, and have deep experience with several of them. It turns out rarely to be fair to have a user deeply skilled in one platform recommend software in a different platform. Sometimes strategies and, therefore, tools are very different between platforms. Daniel Costello and Kendall Hartley, teachers and graduate students who work daily in the Wintel world but take courses with me in the Mac world, have developed "equivalent" lists for inclusion in this section.

Software information is extremely dynamic. There may be inaccuracies in this list. Web addresses may change. As we went to press, there were waves of new products being released and announced.

*Adobe Acrobat*

Takes file from a word processor and converts it into a file that can be read/edited by related products in this family. Any person on any platform with a (freeware) reader can read files encoded in the Acrobat format (.pdf). Files can be searched, hypertext linked, and animated. <http://www.adobe.com/prodindex/main.html> {Available for Mac, Windows, and UNIX.}

*Adobe Illustrator*

An early leader in high-end graphics programs with an excellent array of drawing tools. <http://www.adobe.com/prodindex/main.html> {Available for Mac and Windows.}

*Apple LAN Utility*

Interrogates current machine to determine its ethernet address. Performs function similar to *Get My Address*. In DOS, Windows, and OS/2 worlds, run diagnostics program that comes with ethernet card. Also see *Get My Address*. Provided with Mac OS. Can be downloaded from unsupported utilities folders at Apple download sites.

*Apple Video Player*

Software for capturing movies and stills from the video in port of a Macintosh AV computer. The software is provided with the operating system at the time of purchase.

*Astound*

This is an elegant presentation program along the lines of *Persuasion* and *PowerPoint*. <http://www.astoundinc.com/> {Available for Mac and Windows.}

*Authorware*

A cross-platform multimedia program for Mac and Windows. <http://www.macromedia.com/software/> {Available for Mac and Windows.}

*BBEdit*

*BBEdit* is a text editing program available from Barebones software. This program has become my HTML tagging program of choice. Many tools simplify the tagging process. There is no file size limit. Many files may be kept open simultaneously. HTML tags may be colored for easy editing. Most of all, the tools accomplish much of the busywork of text tagging. For example, when an image is imported, the tool will create an address and also indicate the image's size. By indicating the size of an image, text loads quickly with appropriate space properly reserved for the image for subsequent loading. {In the Windows world, page authors speak highly of (http://www.sausage.com). *Hot Dog Pro* may be more like *PageMill* than *BBEdit*.} <http://www.barebones.com/> {Mac only.}

*Canvas*

*Canvas* is a high-end drawing program for professional illustrators. <http://www.deneba.com/> {Available for Mac and Windows.}

*Chem3D*

*Chem3D* is a molecular modeling and analysis program used by chemists. <http://www.camsci.com/> {Available for Mac and Windows.}

*ChemAnimations*

Filled with animations created for use during an NSF-supported project in teaching AP Chemistry by Satellite, this best-selling CD-ROM for teachers provides excellent means for illustrating molecular concepts. SYNAPS@LTEC.NET {Mac only.}

*ChemDraw*

*ChemDraw* is a chemical structure drawing program, often sold together with *Chem3D*. < http://www.camsci.com/> {Available for Mac and Windows.}

*Chemintosh*

A chemical structure drawing program. <http://www.softshell.com/> {Available for Mac and Windows.}

## Chime

A Netscape plug-in that facilitates viewing chemical structures in three dimensions.  <http://www.mdli.com/chemscape/chime/chime.html>  {Available for several platforms besides Macintosh.}

## ChitChat

A program supporting chat sessions in which on-line users contribute text, can share a whiteboard, and can contribute images.  Similar to *RoundTable*. (*"PowWow* is a unique Internet program for Windows that allows up to seven people to chat, send and receive files, and cruise the World Wide Web together as a group.  Version 2.3 adds color text conferencing and lots of other improvements!"  http://tribal.com/powwow.)  <http://www.mstay.com/>  {Mac only.}

## Claris HomePage

*HomePage* is a WYSIWYG HTML file editor.  The user is able to create an entity on the screen that looks as it would when served over the WWW via an http operation.  Competitive programs are *PageMill* and *PageSpinner*. <http://www.claris.com/>  {Available for Mac and Windows.}

## ClarisWorks

*ClarisWorks* is an integrated program that affords word processing, spreadsheet, graphics, and other functions in one package.  This program, similar to *Microsoft Works*, is popular in schools.  <http://www.claris.com/>  {Available for Mac and Windows.}

## Coda

Developed in Java by a new startup company, Random Noise, and shown in alpha version at the January 1997 MacWorld Expo, this application creates entire Web pages as Java applets.  {Promised to be available for Mac and Windows.}

## CompactPro

A shareware program for lossless compressing of files.  Accomplishes same sorts of tasks as *StuffIt*.  {For expanding *CompactPro* archives on Wintel machines, try *ExtractorPC*, http://www.winsite.com/info/pc/win3/util/ext-pc.zip/.}   < http://hyperarchive.lcs.mit.edu/HyperArchive.html>

## CU-SeeMe

A freeware program for sharing videoimages between two computers.  Can be enhanced making several connections possible concurrently using "reflectors." <http://goliath.wpine.com/cu-seeme.html>  {Available for Mac and Windows.}

## Debabelizer

*Debabelizer* is a utility that interconverts images files from nearly any useful format into nearly any other useful format.    <http://www.equilibrium.com> {Available for Mac and Windows.}

## DeltaGraph

*DeltaGraph* is a graphing program for creating graphs from raw data. It has many attractive curve fitting features. This program also servers as a presentation program (like *PowerPoint* and *Persuasion*). Like its competitors, the program has been retooled for WWW use.    <http://www.deltapoint.com/> {Available for Mac and Windows.}

## Director (Macromedia)

A high-quality animation program that runs files on several platforms. Very high-quality visuals possible. One of the strongest interactive multimedia programs available. <http://www.macromedia.com/software/> {Create and/or play in Macintosh or Windows. See *Shockwave* for *Director*-created materials delivered over the WWW.}

## Elastic Reality

"Elastic Reality is a powerful special effects system combining the most advanced warping and morphing technology available with sophisticated 2D & 3D animation, color correction, matte generation and compositing tools." <http://www.avid.com/products/effects/er/ index.html>    {Available for Mac, Windows, and SGI.}

## Eudora Pro

*Eudora* is an e-mail program. Like *Netscape Navigator*, its roots are in federally funded projects at the University of Illinois. *Eudora* is a very powerful program with many useful features. The *Pro* version that I use allows filtering of incoming e-mail. This allows me to receive mail from listservs that I might otherwise find burdensome. Also, I can quickly create aliases that appear in menus for mailing to individuals and groups, a real time saver. I have such aliases for all of my classes. <http://www.qualcomm.com/> {Available for Mac, Windows, and Newton.}

## Explorer

The Microsoft WWW browser similar to *Netscape Navigator*. <http://www.microsoft.com> {Various Macintosh and Windows versions are available.}

## FaceIt

DOS-based security software that compares images from video to data files of facial images for positive identifications. <http://venezia.rockefeller.edu/faceit/>. {For SGI and possibly DOS.}.

## FileMaker Pro

A powerful relational database program. <http://www.claris.com> {Available for Mac and Windows.}

### Flash-It!

*Flash-It!* is a freeware control panel for Macintosh used to capture screens or portions of screens. *SnagIt* is a similar software package for Windows. Mac Shareware. <http://hyperarchive.lcs.mit.edu/HyperArchive.html>

### FreeHand

*FreeHand* is a high-end drawing program for professional illustrators. <http://www.macromedia.com/software/> {Available for Mac and Windows.}

### Get My Address

This simple freeware program is used to obtain information about a computer's addresses. See *Apple LAN Utility*. Comparable software is available for most systems; the software comes with utilities as part of an ethernet board or device. Mac Shareware. < http://hyperarchive.lcs.mit.edu/HyperArchive.html>

### GIF Converter

Shareware for interconverting image formats. Images pasted from clipboard may be saved in GIF or JPEG formats. Mac Shareware. <http://hyperarchive.lcs.mit.edu/HyperArchive.html>

### HyperCard

The first hypermedia program ever developed by Apple and released in late 1987. Hypertext links to small amounts of text, visual, and sound information. A terrific application in which to create and test model interfaces before committing programming resources. < http://www.devcatalog.apple.com> {Mac Only.}

### Internet Assistant for MS Word

Takes MS *Word 6* files and creates an html-tagged document from them. <http://www.microsoft.com> {Available for Mac and Windows.}

### KaleidaGraph

*KaleidaGraph* creates graphs from raw data. It includes a variety of curve fitting and display features. Like *DeltaGraph Pro*, this is a power graphing program for technically oriented work. <http://www.synergy.com/> {Available for Mac and Windows.}

### KeyServer

"An administrator can install license control into any existing program and then make it freely available site-wide. The most common license types including concurrent-use, zone restricted, and individual user licenses are easily managed. Users get the convenience and performance of stand-alone applications while the KeyServer provides central license management, usage logging, and access security." <http://www.sassafras.com/> {Available for Mac and Windows.}

*ListStar*

Sold by the same company that handles *WebStar*, *ListStar* is intended to handle listservs. <http://www.starnine.com/> {Mac only.}

*LiveCard*

Run *HyperCard* stacks over the WWW using this application. This is a new and potentially very powerful tool. <http://www.interedu.com/royalsoftware /livecard.html> {Mac only.}

*Lotus Notes*

*Notes* has been around for a long time. It has served as a communications program within organizations. It differs from e-mail in the kinds of options it affords. Recent versions have been upgraded for use on the Internet. (One potential advantage/drawback is that the server for the program must reside on a Wintel computer.) Several Net/Web products were being released by Lotus as this book went to press. <http://www.lotus.com> {Available for Mac and Windows.}

*MacHTTP*

An early shareware program for WWW serving. Has evolved into *WebStar*. Mac Shareware. <http://hyperarchive.lcs.mit.edu/HyperArchive.html>

*MailTo Tamer*

Takes pasted text of files encoded for mailing over WWW and decodes them into readable language (English). Mac Shareware. <http://hyperarchive.lcs.mit. edu/HyperArchive.html >

*Maple*

A symbolic algebra program. Permits symbolic manipulation of mathematical equations. <http://www.maplesoft.com/> {Available for Mac, OS/2, and Windows.}

*Mathematica*

A symbolic algebra program. Permits symbolic manipulation of mathematical equations. <http://www.wri.com/> {Available for Mac, Windows, and many other platforms.}

*Mosaic*

The Web browser software that increased interest in the WWW greatly. <http://www.ncsa.uiuc.edu/SDG/Software/Mosaic/> {Available for Mac and Windows.}

*Myrmidon*

A metaprinter that accepts files as if they were being transmitted to a printer and encodes them as html-tagged files. <http://www.terrymorse.com/> {Mac only.}

*NetForms*

Software for creating forms where inputs are posted to a Web site. Used to run discussion groups. Client browser shows forms; input processed at Mac-based server. < http://www.maxum.com> {Mac only.}

*Netscape Navigator*

*Netscape Navigator* is a WWW browser. It has Macintosh, Windows, and other versions. This program, intellectually derived from federally funded *Mosaic*, gave impetus to WWW development. Judging from the various deals announced by Netscape, this program evolves on a near-semiannual basis with more features and power emerging with every cycle. <http://www.netscape.com/> {Available for Mac and Windows.}

*Netscape Navigator Gold*

*Navigator Gold* is essentially *Navigator* with WYSIWYG HTML editing features included. <http://www.netscape.com/> {Available for Mac and Windows.}

*Nisus Writer*

*Nisus Writer* is an often-overlooked word processing program with special features aimed at making document creation for different languages easy. <http://www.nisus-soft.com/> {Mac only.}

*OmniPage Professional*

*OmniPage* is optical character recognition software. When printed text is available that is to be converted (back) into an electronic file format, the pages are scanned using an optical scanner under the control of a program such as *OmniPage*. These program use complex formulas to take the pictures of individual characters and interpret them as alphameric characters. Though done quickly by experienced readers under very trying situations, this remains quite a challenge for computers. <http://www.caere.com/> {Available for Mac and Windows.}

*PageMaker*

A desktop publishing program. <http://www.adobe.com/prodindex/main.html> {Available for Mac and Windows.}

*PageMill*

*PageMill* is a WYSIWYG program for creating HTML files. <http://www.adobe.com/prodindex/main.html> {Mac only.}

*PageSpinner*

*PageSpinner* is a Macintosh HTML shareware text editor. It seems to have about the same kind of power and functionality as does *BBEdit* for this task. Mac Shareware. < http://hyperarchive.lcs.mit.edu/HyperArchive.html>

*Persuasion*

A quality presentation program along the lines of *Astound* and *PowerPoint*. <http://www.adobe.com/prodindex/main.html> {Available for Mac and Windows.}

*Photoshop*

A very high-quality image editing program. For editing photos and similar images. <http://www.adobe.com/prodindex/main.html> {Available for Mac, Windows, SGI, and Sun.}

*PowerPoint*

A quality presentation program along the lines of *Persuasion* and *Astound*. <http://www.microsoft.com> {Available for Mac and Windows.}

*Quark*

A page setting program like *PageMaker* for desktop publishing. <http://www.quark.com/> {Mac only.}

*QuickTime*

An extension of the Macintosh operating system, *QuickTime* is a timing protocol that permits a wide variety of time-based media formats to be integrated into applications and displayed/played on a personal computer. *QuickTime* currently is available for media replay on both Mac and Windows machines, and recent announcements suggest that it will be possible to create materials on either platform as well. In addition, *QuickTime* handles image compression/decompression tasks. <http://www.devcatalog.apple.com>

*QuickTime VR*

*QuickTime* for handling virtual reality images. <http://www.devcatalog.apple.com>

*QuickTime VR Authoring Tools Suite 1.0*

Tools for creating *QuickTime VR* files. <http://www.devcatalog.apple.com>

*Roadster*

Netscape plug-in to run *SuperCard* programs on the WWW. <http://www.allegiant.com/> {Mac current; Windows promised.}

*RoundTable*

A program supporting chat sessions in which on-line users contribute text, can share a whiteboard, and can contribute images. <http://www.ffg.com/> {Available for Mac and Windows. Client free. Windows only server sold.}

*Shockwave*

Netscape plug-in to run *Director* programs on the WWW. <http://www.macromedia.com/software/> {Available for Mac, Windows, and other platforms.}

*SimpleText*

A very simple word processing program provided as freeware with Macintosh computers. Usually used for read-me files and other information provided by suppliers.

*Stoichiometer*

A *HyperCard*-based program for performing chemical bookkeeping calculations. Provides context-specific tutoring after solving problems. <http://www.cci.unl. edu/Chemistry/Commercial_Software/Commercial_Software.html>          {Mac only.}

*StuffIt*

A commercial program for lossless compressing of files. Accomplishes same sorts of tasks as *CompactPro*. A portion of this package, *StuffIt Expander*, is distributed as freeware. The expander is used as a helper with browser software such as *Navigator*. <http://www.aladdinsys.com/index.html> {Mac only.}

*SuiteSpot*

A set of server options offered by Netscape meeting nearly any need. <http://home.netscape.com/comprod/server_central/product/suite_spot/index .html> {Available for Windows NT and UNIX.}

*SuperCard*

*SuperCard* is a hypermedia like *HyperCard*. *SuperCard* has a scripting language (SuperTalk), and uses more predefined objects than does *HyperCard*. *SuperCard* has carefully integrated color throughout. It was originally created by the makers of *SuperPaint*. Many successful multimedia projects have been authored in *SuperCard*. <http://www.allegiant.com/> {Mac only.}

*SuperPaint*

An early program for Macintosh, *SuperPaint* is a combined painting and drawing program. It is still my program of choice, even though there are many other more powerful options these days.   <http://www.adobe.com/prodindex/main .html > {Mac only.}

*Tango*

The Tango Application Server (CGI) links a Macintosh-based Web server to *FileMaker* databases. <http://www.everyware.com> {Mac only.}

*Timbuktu*

*Timbuktu* allows users at one computer to control remotely a different computer. With the proper version of *Timbuktu*, you can log onto your server from home or from a distant location and control that computer. *Timbuktu* is sometimes used in teaching or workplace situations to permit teachers or supervisors to control student or worker computers. <http://www.farallon.com/> {Available for Mac and Windows.}

*Toast*

Controls creation of CD-ROMs in many formats. This software is highly recommended if you want to make hybrid ROMs. <http://194.121.104.60/English/Toast3E/ToProdukte.html> {Mac only.}

*ToolBook*

Windows-based hypermedia program akin to *HyperCard* and *SuperCard*. *ToolBook* uses a plug-in called *Neuron* to make programs available on the WWW. < http://www.asymetrix.com/solutions.html > {Windows only.}

*Transparency*

Create transparent pixels in GIF images with *Transparency*. Mac Shareware. <http://hyperarchive.lcs.mit.edu/HyperArchive.html>

*Videoshop*

*Videoshop* handles nonlinear desktop television editing. <http://www.strata3d.com/> {Mac only.}

*Visual Cafe*

A remarkable development tool for the creation of Java applications. The code for objects created in one window appears in a second window. Changing the code in the code window leads directly to changes in the properties of the object. Symantec has a history of creating excellent development tools for the C++ language. <http://www.symantec.com> {Available for Mac, Windows95, and Windows NT.}

*Visual Page*

A WYSIWYG application from Symantec for creating HTML- tagged Web pages. Although a late entry to the field, this program shows enormous promise. <http://www.symantec.com> {Mac only.}

*WebBurst*

This application creates flashy Java applets for inclusion within Web pages. <http://www.powerproduction.com> {Mac only.}

*WebStar*

*WebStar*, a marvelous sequel to Chuck Shotton's *MacHTTP*, is one of the easiest programs I've ever used. With *WebStar*, setting up a Macintosh as a WWW server is about a 5-minute operation. Essentially, you start the program (double click the icon), and that's all! <http://www.starnine.com/> {Mac only.}

*WebWhacker*

Copy all files (html, images) from a Web site. Numerous commercial (and at least one shareware) products are emerging that perform these tasks. <http://www.ffg.com/> {Available for Mac and Windows.}

*Word*

Microsoft *Word* is a full-service word processor. Version 6.01 (Mac) was used to prepare the manuscript for this book.    <http://www.microsoft.com> {Available for Mac and Windows.}

*WordPerfect*

*WordPerfect* is a full-service word processor. It has been a major competitor to *Word*.    <http://www.corel.com/products/wordperfect/index.htm>    {Runs on many platforms including Mac and Windows.}

# URLs

URL A. (http://monarch.bio.ukans.edu/). Monarch Watch.

URL B. (http://www.boutell.com/boutell/png/). PNG (Portable Network Graphics) Specification.

URL C. (http://www.cc.gatech.edu/gvu/user_surveys/survey-04-1996/graphs/webmaster/server.html). GVU's Fifth WWW User Survey Server Graphs.

URL D. (http://www.mcp.com/hayden/iskm/book.html). Internet Starter Kit.

URL E. (http://www.allegiant.com/roadster/). Allegiant Roadster Home Page.

URL F. (http://www.netscape.com/comprod/at_work/ white_ paper/intranet/vision.html#fullserve). Netscape Intranet Product Line.

URL G. (http://www.farallon.com/www/catalog/cattb2m.html). Farallon Product Catalog: Timbuktu Pro Macintosh.

URL H. (http://www.gta.com/firewall.html). GFX Internet Firewall System.

URL J. (http://www.virtus.com/3dwb.html). Virtus Corporation: 3-D Website Builder.

URL K. (http://home.netscape.com/eng/mozilla/Gold/handbook/ plugins/ad2.html). Netscape: Architecture.

URL L. (http://www.macweek.com/mw_1018/sr_tech.html). Special Report: MacWeek Guide to Digital Imaging.

URL M. (http://www.colby.edu/chemistry/OChem/ STEREO-CHEM/index.html). Stereochemistry Online.

URL N. (http://www.mdli.com/prod/chemscape/index.html). Chemscape Main Page.

URL O. (http://www.colby.edu/chemistry/OChem/STEREOCHEM/ index.html). Stereochemistry Online.

URL P. (http://hyperarchive.lcs.mit.edu/HyperArchive.html). INFO-MAC HyperArchive Root.

URL Q. (http://freenet.msp.mn.us/people/drwool/webconf.html). Computer Conferencing on the Web (Discussion Forums and Groupware).

URL R. (http://www.maxum.com/NFStart.html). Welcome to NetForms!

URL S. (http://www.starnine.com/webstar/overview.html). SUMMARY: A Model of Web Server Performance.

URL T. (http://www.interedu.com/heizer/livecard.html). Introducing Live-Card!: Page 1.

URL U. (http://www.macweek.com/mw_1035/news_hypercard .html). News: HyperCard's new deal: QuickTime authoring.

URL V. (http://www.mstay.com/ch10_ab1.html#). ChitChat: Instant Multi-media Communication.

URL W. (http://128.59.113.173/wwwnjt/Links/Organic/ Organic1.html). Or-ganic Chemistry. (Course site for Professor Nicholas Turro, Columbia Uni-versity.)

URL X. (http://www.adobe.com/prodindex/premiere/ overview.html). Adobe Premiere Overview.

URL Y. (http://www.sun.com/products-n-solutions/hw/wstns/ index.html). Sun Microsystems Products Page: SPARCstation Family.

URL Z. (http://www.discmfg.com/index.html). Disc Manufacturing, Inc.

URL AA. (http://venezia.rockefeller.edu/faceit/). The FaceIt Homepage.

URL AB. (http://crc-sybase.unl.edu/cgi-bin/Notebooks). sineDemo.nb.

URL AC. (http://www.mc.maricopa.edu/academic/phy_sci/Chemistry/faculty /dorland/chime.html). Chemistry Tutorial and Resource Page.

URL AD. (http://www.mapquest.com/). MapQuest! Welcome!

URL AE. (http://www.yahoo.com/). Yahoo!

URL AF. (http://sulcus.berkeley.edu/mcb165/). MCB165 WWW Neurochem-istry Site.

URL AG. (http://www.interedu.com/livecard.cgi). LC Home.

URL AH. (http://www.yahoo.com/Computers/Multimedia/). Yahoo! - Com-puters and Internet:Multimedia.

URL AJ. (http://www.raspberryhill.com/gifwizard.html). GIF Wizard from Raspberry Hill Publishing.

URL AK.  (http://itech1.coe.uga.edu/EPSS/EPSS.html).  EPSS Resources
    Home Page.

URL AL.  (http://www-dsed.llnl.gov/documents/wwwtest.html).  WWW
    Viewer Test Page.

URL AM.  (http://www.apstech.com/).  APS Home Page.

# INDEX